Purpose
Companies
for Social Good

Hiroko Harada
Maiko Tsuchiya
Samantha Hawkins

KINSEIDO

JN125949

Kinseido Publishing Co., Ltd.

3-21 Kanda Jimbo-cho, Chiyoda-ku,
Tokyo 101-0051, Japan

Copyright © 2024 by Hiroko Harada
                     Maiko Tsuchiya
                     Samantha Hawkins

*All rights reserved. No part of this publication may
be reproduced, stored in a retrieval system, or transmitted,
in any form or by any means, electronic, mechanical,
photocopying, recording or otherwise, without the prior
permission of the publisher.*

First published 2024 by Kinseido Publishing Co., Ltd.

Design: Nampoosha Co., Ltd.
Illustrations: Toru Igarashi

 音声ファイル無料ダウンロード

https://www.kinsei-do.co.jp/download/4199

この教科書で DL 00 の表示がある箇所の音声は、上記 URL または QR コードにて
無料でダウンロードできます。自習用音声としてご活用ください。

▶ PC からのダウンロードをお勧めします。スマートフォンなどでダウンロードされる場合は、
　ダウンロード前に「解凍アプリ」をインストールしてください。
▶ URL は、検索ボックスではなくアドレスバー (URL 表示欄) に入力してください。
▶ お使いのネットワーク環境によっては、ダウンロードできない場合があります。

◎ CD 00　左記の表示がある箇所の音声は、教室用 CD（Class Audio CD）に収録されています。

はじめに

　本書は、学生の皆さんが日常生活の中でよく目にする14の企業を取り上げ、それらの企業が社会をよりよくするために行っている取り組みに注目しました。これから社会に出る皆さんに、このテキストを通じて企業と社会の関わりについて理解しながら、英語学習を深めてほしいと思います。

　各ユニットで取り上げた企業の業種は、製造業、小売業、情報通信業、飲食サービス業など、どれも身近に感じる業種だと思います。企業の仕事や活動について考えるとき、皆さんはどのようなことを想像しますか？　一人の客として企業と接すると、食品メーカーは食品を製造・販売し、小売りスーパーは商品を仕入れて売り場に陳列する……そして皆さんはそれらの商品を購入する、ということを思い浮かべるかもしれません。しかしながら、企業は、その業種に関わることだけに力を注いでいるわけではありません。例えば、ある食品メーカーは、食品を製造・販売するだけでなく、食を通じて子どもたちに環境問題を考える機会を設けたり、運動をする楽しさを伝え健康を促進する働きかけを行ったりしています。また、ある電気機器メーカーは、エンジニアを育てるために教育機関の充実に乗り出しています。このように、企業はよりよい社会やコミュニティを創るために独自の活動を行っているのです。

　主に各ユニットのリーディングパートで、このような企業の社会的取り組みを紹介しています。まず、リーディングパートをしっかりと理解できるように、学習の導入として必要な単語や熟語の習得、事前の企業調査を行ってください。リーディングパートで企業の取り組みについて理解した後は、会話や作文を行い、英語の知識を定着させながら、自分の英語で企業の取り組みを表現できるようになりましょう。そして、ユニット全体を通して、「この会社はこんな活動をしていたんだ」と企業の新たな顔を知ることによって、日常生活の中で企業や店舗、商品を見る目に変化が起こることを望んでいます。

　このテキストのタイトルである "Purpose" には「社会の中における企業の存在意義」や「（企業の）意志」に加え、「（学生の皆さんが学ぶ）目的」という意味が込められています。本書を通して、社会をよくするための企業の「存在意義」や「意志」を理解し、「自分だったらこんな取り組みで社会に貢献したい」という皆さんの「目的」を見つけてください。

著者一同

本書の使い方

Small Chat

各ユニットの学習を始める際に、ペアまたはグループで英語を使ったウォームアップをします。質問には皆さんのアイデアを自由に答えてもいいですし、回答に困ったときは右側の選択肢を使って答えることもできます。選択肢の語句だけではなく、センテンスで答えるようにすると英会話力の向上につながります。自分の回答をグレーの解答欄に書いたら、周りのクラスメートと英語でやりとりをしましょう。

Words and Phrases

A 日本語の内容を表す英語のスペルを書き、この後の **Speed Reading** で役立つ単語を覚えましょう。スペルが分からないときは、まず自分で調べて書いてみましょう。すべてを記入したら、今度は音声を聞きながら声に出して発音を確認しましょう。アクセントの箇所にマークをつけるなどの工夫もするとよいでしょう。

B この後の **Speed Reading** で役に立つフレーズの意味を確認しましょう。その後、**A** と同様に音声を活用しましょう。

Dictation

Speed Reading の学習を始める前に書き取りの練習をします。音声を聞き、空所に入る語を書き入れましょう。単語のスペルが分からないときは、分かる範囲で書くようにし、全くの空欄とならないようにするのが、リスニング力を上げるコツです(例："dictation" のスペルが分からないが、最初の音はなんとなく分かる場合、"di___" のように書いておきましょう)。音声は繰り返し聞いてもよいです。また、解答を確認した後に、再度音声を聞き、聞き取れなかった音を確認することも英語の耳を作るのにとても大切です。

Pre-knowledge

まとまった英文を読む前に、関連する知識を確認することは英語のリーディング力をつけるのに有効です。企業についての英文が正しいのかどうか、キーワードを取り出して検索してみましょう。例えば、There are about 200 million LINE users and most of them are American. という文については、「LINE、利用者、国別」などがキーワードになるでしょう。調べた情報は、**Speed Reading** での皆さんの読解に役に立ちますのでメモを残しておきましょう。

Speed Reading

このセクションでは、皆さんのリーディング力を高めるためにスピードリーディングというトレーニングをします。必要な情報を即座に捉える力は社会で求められるものです。手元にスマートフォンや腕時計などのストップウォッチで時間を計る準備をし、緊張感をもって取り組みましょう。音読できた時間を計ったら、*Speed Records* に記録をし、wpm を算出しましょう。wpm は "Words per minute"（１分間に読める語数)のことです。160語程度を目指すとよいでしょう。読むスピードを上げつつ、分からない発音もチェックすることで、確実にリスニング力とリーディング力が上がります。各種資格試験の対策として、まず右側の質問に目を通し、情報を的確に捉えることを意識しながら左側の英文を読むのも効果的です。１つの段落を読み終えるごとに、右側の質問に答えましょう。

Dialog

A 音声を聞きながら空所を埋めます。**Dictation** と同様に、分かる範囲で聞こえた音を書くように心がけましょう。

B スピーキング力とリスニング力を上げるためのトレーニングです。**STEP 1 → STEP 5** の順番で進めましょう。

STEP 1 発音が分からないと、知っている単語も聞こえないものです。リスニング力を上げるために発音が分からない語には下線を引きましょう。

STEP 2 下線を引いた個所に注意しながら音声を聞きましょう。

STEP 3 ペアで声に出して読みながら、自分の発音を確認しましょう。

STEP 4 & **STEP 5** 英語を読める速さは聞き取れる速さに比例します。ネイティブスピーカーと同じスピードで読むことに挑戦しましょう。１回の練習では難しい場合もあります。繰り返しの練習が大切です。

Expression A B

アウトプットの練習です。これまでの学習を振り返りながら、ユニットで学習した表現を定着させ、最後には自分の意見を書きましょう。

Contents

7-ELEVEN

地域密着の移動販売車

Small Chat

右の語句を参考に、次の問いに答えましょう。

What do you usually buy at convenience stores?

1.

How close is the nearest convenience store to your house?

2.

Have you ever used a mobile food van?

3.

| rice balls |

| a 10-minute walk |

| have never used one |

| candy |

| use one sometimes |

| a 20-minute walk |

Words and Phrases

 DL 002   CD1-02

A 次の日本語に合う英語を（　　）内に書き入れましょう。

1. フランチャイズ式の　　(f _ _ _ _ _ _ _ _ _ _)

2. 〜を強調する　　(s _ _ _ _ _ _)

3. 近所　　(n _ _ _ _ _ _ _ _ _ _ _ _)

4. 驚くことに　　(s _ _ _ _ _ _ _ _ _ _ _ _)

5. 〜を強調する　　(e _ _ _ _ _ _ _ _ _)

6. さらに　　(f _ _ _ _ _ _ _ _ _ _)

7. 料理　　(d _ _ _)

8. 地域　　(r _ _ _ _ _)

9. 香味料　　(f _ _ _ _ _ _ _ _)

10. なじみのある　　(f _ _ _ _ _ _ _)

B 次の語句に合う日本語訳を選択肢から選びましょう。

1. as of ~   (   )   **a.** ～によって、～次第で

2. connect with ~   (   )   **b.** 地域コミュニティ

3. local community   (   )   **c.** ～時点で

4. unique characteristic   (   )   **d.** ～とつながりを持つ

5. depending on ~   (   )   **e.** 独特の特徴

Dictation

🎧 DL 003   💿 CD1-03

音声を聞いて空所を埋めましょう。その後、英文を日本語に訳しましょう。

1. "Time convenience" was (   ) at first.

   _____

2. Some elderly people have trouble finding stores in the (   ).

   _____

3. The company aims to (   ) with the (   ) (   ).

   _____

Pre-knowledge

セブン-イレブンについて調べ、次の1～3が正しければT、間違っていればFを選びましょう。調べた際に、新たに知ったことがあればメモ欄に書き留めましょう。

1. The first Seven-Eleven store opened in the U.S. in 1927.   [T / F]

2. Some Seven-Eleven stores play the role of a fire station.   [T / F]

3. Seven-Eleven is working on "Chisan Chisho" (local production and consumption).

   [T / F]

Speed Reading

次の英文はA～Cの3段落に分かれています。以下のステップに沿って進めましょう。

STEP 1 英文を読み、段落ごとにタイムを計りましょう。読むのにかかった時間とWPM（1分あたりに読める語数）を右の **Speed Records** に記録しましょう。

STEP 2 英文を再度読みましょう。段落を読み終えるごとに、右の問いに答えましょう。

A **55 words** 🎧 DL 004 ◎ CD1-04

    Seven-Eleven was the first franchised convenience store in Japan and opened its first store in Tokyo in 1974. As of 2023, Seven-Eleven has more than 21,000 stores across Japan. At first, Seven-Eleven stressed "time convenience" when it started to open 24/7, but now it is expanding its business interests to connect with
5 the local community.

B **75 words** 🎧 DL 005 ◎ CD1-05

    For example, Seven-Eleven supports people without stores for shopping in the neighborhood or the elderly who cannot go out far. Seven-Eleven staff drive a mobile food van with about 300 products, from ice cream to rice balls, and sell them to such people. Seven-Eleven also plays the role of a "safety station." It helps
10 kids, women, and the elderly when they are in trouble. Surprisingly, Seven-Eleven helped such people more than 18,000 times in 2021.

C **116 words** 🎧 DL 006 ◎ CD1-06

    To connect with the local community, food is also an important factor. Seven-Eleven emphasizes the following cycle: buying ingredients from local producers, making products using them, and then selling them to the community.
15 Furthermore, it creates original dishes based on local food cultures. For example, noodles have unique characteristics depending on the place. Each region has its own flavoring. The taste of the toppings is also different. People living in East Japan might be surprised when they eat the udon or soba of Kyushu. Seven-Eleven receives information from the locals and develops dishes familiar to them so they
20 can enjoy the taste and feel happy. To be a "community store" is a new theme for Seven-Eleven.

Speed Records

Ⓐ 55（語数）÷ _____（かかった秒数）× **60**（1分あたり）= _____ wpm

Ⓑ 75（語数）÷ _____（かかった秒数）× **60**（1分あたり）= _____ wpm

Ⓒ 116（語数）÷ _____（かかった秒数）× **60**（1分あたり）= _____ wpm

Ⓐ

1. セブン-イレブンは日本で最初のどのような形態のお店でしたか。（　　　　　　　　　　　）

2. 1974年にセブン-イレブンの店舗数は21,000でしたか。　　　　　　（はい・いいえ）

3. 開業当初セブン-イレブンが重視していたのはどのような考えでしたか。

（　　　　　　　　　　　）

Ⓑ

1. セブン-イレブンは近所に（　　　　　　　　　　　）がない人々をサポートしています。

2. セブン-イレブンの移動販売車には約（　　　　　　　　）が載っています。

3. セブン-イレブンは街の（　　　　　　　　　　）として困っている人々をサポートしています。

Ⓒ

1. Seven-Eleven tries to connect with local people through food. **[T / F]**

2. Different types of noodles, flavors, and toppings are found in various regions.

[T / F]

3. Seven-Eleven only focuses on original dishes made in the Kyushu style. **[T / F]**

Dialog

A 次の会話を聞き、空所にあてはまる語を書き入れましょう。　🎧 DL 007　◎ CD1-07

Emma: I've been loving this chocolate cake from Seven-Eleven. I always buy this after class.

Kento: I know, it's so ¹·(　　　　　　). I called my grandmother the other day, and she said she loved it, too.

Emma: Oh, good. How is she doing? Does your grandmother live by herself?

Kento: Yes. She lives in the countryside. Surprisingly, there are no stores in her neighborhood, but she buys the cakes from a ²·(　　　　　　) ³·(　　　　　) ⁴·(　　　　　). It's quite convenient.

Emma: For sure! I like the idea. Many people who have trouble with shopping will surely find it useful.

Kento: It's really amazing that ⁵·(　　　　　　　　) ⁶·(　　　　　　) make an effort to serve people in all regions.

B 次の1〜5のステップで、会話の発話練習をしましょう。

STEP 1 ▷ 音読し、発音が分からない単語に下線を引きましょう。

STEP 2 ▷ **A**の音声をもう一度聞いて、発音を確認しましょう。

STEP 3 ▷ ペアを組み、EmmaとKentoになって読んでみましょう。

STEP 4 ▷ Emmaのみの音声（🎧 DL 008　◎ CD1-08 ）を聞き、音声のスピードを意識しながらKentoのパートを発話しましょう。

STEP 5 ▷ Kentoのみの音声（🎧 DL 009　◎ CD1-09 ）を聞き、音声のスピードを意識しながらEmmaのパートを発話しましょう。

Expression

A 日本語訳を参考に、英文を完成させましょう。

1. The number of convenience stores in Japan is about 57,000 _____

   _____.

   日本のコンビニエンスストアの数は、**2023年時点で**約57,000です。

2. The children in this town usually help _____

   _____.

   この町の子どもたちは、普段から**困っているお年寄り**を助けています。

3. _____ in the new

   university.

   その新しい大学には**いくつかの独特の特徴があります**。

4. _____ his idea.

   驚くことに、彼は自分の考え**を強調しました。**

B セブン-イレブンについて自分の意見を書いてみましょう。

What's your view on Seven-Eleven?

I think Seven-Eleven is a/an _____ company

because _____.

セブン-イレブンのロゴデザイン

　セブン-イレブンのロゴマークは、オレンジと赤で彩られた数字の「7」の上に「ELEVEn」の文字が緑で書かれていますが、皆さんは最後の「n」だけが、小文字の字体になっていることを知っていましたか？　ほかの大文字と大きさが変わらない「n」なので、一見気づきにくいですが、よく見ると小文字になっています。なぜ最後の「n」だけが小文字なのでしょうか？

　ロゴが発表されたのが70年ほど前のため、確かな資料は残っておらず、その理由については諸説あるそうですが、小文字にして丸みをおびたロゴにすることで、親しみやすさを表現したといわれています。

セブン-イレブンがアメリカのテキサス州で創業したときは、何の販売店だったでしょう？

a. 氷
b. 牛乳
c. パン

Unit 2
LINE

スマホ世代に伝えたい情報リテラシー

Small Chat

右の語句を参考に、次の問いに答えましょう。

What do you use when you communicate with your friends?

> 1.

What is your favorite emoji to use?

> 2.

What's a good way to say, "It's funny!" in text?

> 3.

a smiley face

my phone

a thumbs up

LOL

haha

social media

Words and Phrases

 DL 010　CD1-10

A 次の日本語に合う英語を（　　）内に書き入れましょう。

1. 100万の　　　　(m _ _ _ _ _ _)
2. 必要な　　　　　(n _ _ _ _ _ _ _ _)
3. 教育的な　　　　(e _ _ _ _ _ _ _ _ _ _ _)
4. 安全に　　　　　(s _ _ _ _ _)
5. 適切に　　　　　(a _ _ _ _ _ _ _ _ _ _ _ _)
6. 教材　　　　　　(m _ _ _ _ _ _ _)
7. 助言　　　　　　(t _ _)
8. フレーズ　　　　(p _ _ _ _ _)
9. ユニークな　　　(u _ _ _ _ _)
10. 〜を認識する　　(r _ _ _ _ _ _ _ _)

14

B 次の語句に合う日本語訳を選択肢から選びましょう。

1. general incorporated foundation （　　） **a.** ソーシャルメディア

2. related to ~ （　　） **b.** 一般財団法人

3. social media （　　） **c.** AにBを提供する

4. provide A with B （　　） **d.** 例えば

5. for example （　　） **e.** ～に関連する

Dictation

🎧 DL 011　⊙ CD1-11

音声を聞いて空所を埋めましょう。その後、英文を日本語に訳しましょう。

1. The Internet and social media are (　　　　　　　　) for all ages.

　_____

2. They enjoy the textbook (　　　　　　) (　　　　　　) U.S. culture.

　_____

3. I don't want to hear, "You're (　　　　)" (　　　) (　　　　).

　_____

Pre-knowledge

LINEについて調べ、次の1～3が正しければT、間違っていればFを選びましょう。調べた際に、新たに知ったことがあればメモ欄に書き留めましょう。

1. There are about 200 million LINE users and most of them are American. [T / F]

2. A general incorporated foundation called LINE Mirai Foundation was founded in 2019. [T / F]

3. LINE Mirai Foundation offers educational workshops to students from elementary to high school. [T / F]

Speed Reading

次の英文はA～Cの3段落に分かれています。以下のステップに沿って進めましょう。

STEP 1 英文を読み、段落ごとにタイムを計りましょう。読むのにかかった時間と WPM（1分あたりに読める語数）を右の **Speed Records** に記録しましょう。

STEP 2 英文を再度読みましょう。段落を読み終えるごとに、右の問いに答えましょう。

A 62 words DL 012 CD1-12

As of 2022, about 200 million people use LINE, mainly in Asia. It is popular among a wide range of ages, including teenagers. This is because not only adults, but also young students live in a society where the Internet and social media are necessary. Because of this situation, the general incorporated foundation LINE
5 Mirai Foundation offers educational activities to the young.

B 74 words DL 013 CD1-13

The foundation provides education for young students on how to use the Internet safely and communicate appropriately online. It offers online workshops related to social media use to schools for free. Furthermore, it provides teachers and parents with free materials with safety tips so they can also talk with their
10 students and children about it. LINE Mirai Foundation hopes the young do not get in trouble communicating online and instead can just enjoy communication.

C 116 words DL 014 CD1-14

The materials and tools for its workshops do not simply show examples of Internet troubles. The foundation uses original tools to make students think deeply about communication. For example, students can learn through cards. Each card
15 has a phrase, such as, "You're a good student," "You're quiet," "You do everything well," "You're unique," and "You have your own pace." Then, students place the cards in the order of what they would not want to hear from others and then they compare them with their classmates. They can recognize differences among people and learn we all have different views. LINE Mirai Foundation thinks this is the
20 first step to getting to know each other and communicating well.

Speed Records

A 62 (語数) ÷ _____ (かかった秒数) × **60** (1分あたり) = _____ wpm

B 74 (語数) ÷ _____ (かかった秒数) × **60** (1分あたり) = _____ wpm

C 116 (語数) ÷ _____ (かかった秒数) × **60** (1分あたり) = _____ wpm

A

1. LINEの主なユーザーはどの地域にいますか。　　　　　　　（　　　　　　　　　　）

2. 中学生の間でLINEは人気ですか。　　　　　　　　　　（はい・いいえ）

3. LINEみらい財団は若者に何を提供しますか。　　　　（　　　　　　　　　　）

B

1. LINEみらい財団はインターネットを（　　　　　　　）に、そしてオンラインで適切に（　　　　　　　）をするための教育活動を行っています。

2. LINEみらい財団は（　　　　　　　　　　　）に関連するワークショップを提供しています。

3. LINEみらい財団は無料の（　　　　　　）を（　　　　　　　　）や保護者に提供しています。

C

1. The foundation uses activities to help students think more about conversation.

[T / F]

2. The foundation helps students practice giving compliments to each other. **[T / F]**

3. People may have different views when hearing a certain phrase. **[T / F]**

Dialog

A 次の会話を聞き、空所にあてはまる語を書き入れましょう。 🎧 DL 015 ⊙ CD1-15

Emma: I ¹·(   ) Mia yesterday to ask if she had finished the homework. I got a reply saying, "I did. Why do you ask me?"

Kento: Hmm .... That ²·(   ) ³·(   ) she was upset that you asked. I wonder why.

Emma: Maybe she thought I didn't expect her to do her homework. I didn't mean that, though.

Kento: Yeah, ⁴·(   ) through text messages is difficult. It's difficult to recognize the other person's intention.

Emma: Right. We can't know the tone of the other person's ⁵·(   ).

Kento: I think talking ⁶·(   ) ⁷·(   ) is sometimes better than texting. It's necessary to tell her that you didn't mean to upset her.

Emma: You're right, I'll talk with her tomorrow. Thanks for the tip!

B 次の１～５のステップで、会話の発話練習をしましょう。

STEP 1 音読し、発音が分からない単語に下線を引きましょう。

STEP 2 Aの音声をもう一度聞いて、発音を確認しましょう。

STEP 3 ペアを組み、EmmaとKentoになって読んでみましょう。

STEP 4 Emmaのみの音声（🎧 DL 016 ⊙ CD1-16 ）を聞き、音声のスピードを意識しながらKentoのパートを発話しましょう。

STEP 5 Kentoのみの音声（🎧 DL 017 ⊙ CD1-17 ）を聞き、音声のスピードを意識しながらEmmaのパートを発話しましょう。

Expression

A 日本語訳を参考に、英文を完成させましょう。

1. I think communicating _____ is easier.

対面での コミュニケーションのほうが簡単だと思います。

2. Free workshops _____ are

popular.

ソーシャルメディアに関連する無料のワークショップは人気があります。

3. _____ online materials.

その先生は学生たちにオンライン教材を提供しました。

4. _____ at the event.

学生たちは人々が異なる考えを持っていることをそのイベントで学びました。

B LINEについて自分の意見を書いてみましょう。

What's your view on LINE?

I think LINE is a/an _____ application

because _____.

LINEの誕生と東日本大震災

　LINEというサービスの誕生には東日本大震災が関係していたことを知っていますか？　震災が起こったとき、多くの地域で水や電気のみならず、電話やメールなどのインフラが使えなくなりました。家族や友達の安否を知りたいのに連絡ができないという状況を多くの人が経験しました。

　そうした中で「こうした時こそ、大切な人と連絡をとることができる手段が必要だ」という想いのもと、LINEというモバイルメッセンジャーが誕生したのです。そして「人と人を結ぶ線」という意味を込めて、このサービスをLINEと名付けました。

LINEの開発当初、開発チームがメッセージングアプリ以外に開発を検討していたアプリはどれでしょう？

a. ゲームアプリ
b. 音楽配信アプリ
c. 写真共有アプリ

※本ユニットの内容は2023年8月時点の情報です。
※LINE株式会社は、グループ内再編に伴い2023年10月1日よりLINEヤフー株式会社となっています。

Unit 3

NISSIN FOODS

笑顔を届ける百福士プロジェクト

Small Chat

右の語句を参考に、次の問いに答えましょう。

What is your favorite flavor of ramen?

> 1.

Do you like any other easy-to-prepare foods?

> 2.

What do you do for the environment?

> 3.

| frozen food |

| tonkotsu flavor |

| instant noodles |

| use eco-friendly goods |

| miso flavor |

| reduce leftovers |

Words and Phrases

 DL 018　◎ CD1-18

A 次の日本語に合う英語を（　　）内に書き入れましょう。

1. 創立者　　　　　　　(f _ _ _ _ _ _)

2. 熱狂的な、熱心な　　(e _ _ _ _ _ _ _ _ _ _ _ _)

3. 独創的な　　　　　　(o _ _ _ _ _ _ _)

4. 〜を組み合わせる　　(c _ _ _ _ _ _)

5. 〜を再発見する　　　(r _ _ _ _ _ _ _ _ _)

6. 身体的な　　　　　　(p _ _ _ _ _ _ _)

7. 〜を提供する　　　　(p _ _ _ _ _ _)

8. 機会　　　　　　　　(o _ _ _ _ _ _ _ _ _ _)

9. 努力　　　　　　　　(e _ _ _ _ _ _)

10. 〜を解決する　　　　(s _ _ _ _)

B 次の語句に合う日本語訳を選択肢から選びましょう。

1. carry out ~   (   )   **a.**   ～が原因で

2. food waste   (   )   **b.**   食品廃棄物

3. carbon emission   (   )   **c.**   炭素排出

4. due to ~   (   )   **d.**   ～を実行する、～を実施する

5. strive to ~   (   )   **e.**   ～しようと努力する

Dictation

🎧 DL 019   ◎ CD1-19

音声を聞いて空所を埋めましょう。その後、英文を日本語に訳しましょう。

1. The (   ) made (   ) to invent the instant noodle.

     _____

2. In one of the projects of NISSIN FOODS Group, children created (   )

     recipes.

     _____

3. Thirty-one projects had been (   ) (   ) by March 2023.

     _____

Pre-knowledge

日清食品について調べ、次の１～３が正しければT、間違っていればFを選びましょう。
調べた際に、新たに知ったことがあればメモ欄に書き留めましょう。

1. NISSIN FOODS Group provides food to areas affected by disaster.   [T / F]

2. The founder of NISSIN FOODS Group was born in 1915.   [T / F]

3. NISSIN FOODS Group does research on cultured meat.   [T / F]

Speed Reading

次の英文はA～Cの3段落に分かれています。以下のステップに沿って進めましょう。

STEP 1 英文を読み、段落ごとにタイムを計りましょう。読むのにかかった時間と WPM（1分あたりに読める語数）を右の **Speed Records** に記録しましょう。

STEP 2 英文を再度読みましょう。段落を読み終えるごとに、右の問いに答えましょう。

A **60 words** 🎧 DL 020 ◎ CD1-20

Momofuku Ando, the founder of NISSIN FOODS Group, invented the world's first instant noodles in 1958. He was enthusiastic about making a better society. Carrying on Ando's vision, NISSIN FOODS Group began the "Hyakufukushi Project," which lists 100 projects to make the future better over 50 years. These
5 projects center on five themes: creation, food, the earth, health, and children.

B **80 words** 🎧 DL 021 ◎ CD1-21

In 2022, the company carried out the "Nissin Eco Chef Project." In this project, children learned about what they could do for the environment through food. Sixty elementary school students participated in this event online. They learned what they could do to reduce food waste and carbon emissions when they bought food
10 and boiled water to make instant noodles. Also, they enjoyed creating original recipes called "Eco-Arranged Menus" by combining instant "Chicken Ramen" with ingredients in the refrigerator at home.

C **115 words** 🎧 DL 022 ◎ CD1-22

In addition, NISSIN FOODS Group carried out the project called "RUN! JUMP! THROW! WAKU-WAKU KIDS" in 2023. This project taught children the
15 importance of eating and exercising, and helped them rediscover the joy of physical activity after spending a long time at home due to the Covid-19 pandemic. At this event, the group invited an Olympic athlete as a guest instructor to provide a talk show and fun opportunities for children to enjoy exercising and learning basic physical movements. By March 2023, the group had carried out 31 projects out of
20 100, and has been engaged in a variety of other efforts striving to solve social and environmental problems in order to sustain continued growth.

<table>
<tr><td rowspan="3">**Speed Records**</td><td>Ⓐ</td><td>60（語数）÷ _____（かかった秒数）× 60（1分あたり）= _____ wpm</td></tr>
<tr><td>Ⓑ</td><td>80（語数）÷ _____（かかった秒数）× 60（1分あたり）= _____ wpm</td></tr>
<tr><td>Ⓒ</td><td>115（語数）÷ _____（かかった秒数）× 60（1分あたり）= _____ wpm</td></tr>
</table>

Ⓐ

1. 1958年に何が発明されましたか。 （   ）

2. 安藤百福は社会を良くするために熱心でしたか。 （はい・いいえ）

3. 百福士プロジェクトのテーマに含まれているものは何ですか。

   a. 平等　　**b.** 創造

Ⓑ

1. 日清食品は子どもたちが（   ）を通して環境を考えるプロジェクトを行っています。

2. 60人の小学生たちが（   ）と（   ）を減らすためにできることを学びました。

3. 子どもたちは、家の（   ）にある（   ）とチキンラーメンを組み合わせて独創的なレシピを作りました。

Ⓒ

1. NISSIN FOODS Group invited an Olympic athlete to teach children about the importance of eating healthy food. **[T / F]**

2. As of March 2023, the group had carried out over half of the projects. **[T / F]**

3. The group focuses on projects only related to the environment. **[T / F]**

Dialog

A 次の会話を聞き、空所にあてはまる語を書き入れましょう。　　🎧 DL 023　◎ CD1-23

Kento: I'm hungry. Why don't we have instant noodles before going to our club activity? Let's ¹·(　　　　　　) some water!

Emma: Good idea! Oh, I thought that Cup Noodles had a ²·(　　　　　　) of tape to hold the lid down, but there isn't one here.

Kento: You're right. Nissin got ³·(　　　　　　) of the tape in 2021 to reduce the use of plastic. It means that they reduce as much as 33 tons of plastic a year!

Emma: Thirty-three tons! That tiny tape really has an impact on the ⁴·(　　　　　　　　　).

Kento: Yes, so the new design has two tabs that can hold the lid down instead.

Emma: That's true. Those two tabs keep the lid down properly and we can eat hot and ⁵·(　　　　　　　) noodles. They are also making efforts to ⁶·(　　　　　) environmental problems.

B 次の１～５のステップで、会話の発話練習をしましょう。

STEP 1 　音読し、発音が分からない単語に下線を引きましょう。

STEP 2 　**A**の音声をもう一度聞いて、発音を確認しましょう。

STEP 3 　ペアを組み、KentoとEmmaになって読んでみましょう。

STEP 4 　Kentoのみの音声（🎧 DL 024　◎ CD1-24 ）を聞き、音声のスピードを意識しながらEmmaのパートを発話しましょう。

STEP 5 　Emmaのみの音声（🎧 DL 025　◎ CD1-25 ）を聞き、音声のスピードを意識しながらKentoのパートを発話しましょう。

Expression

A 日本語訳を参考に、英文を完成させましょう。

1. Momofuku Ando was _____ about improving society.

   安藤百福は社会を良くするために**熱心**でした。

2. Students made a presentation of _____ for

   the environment through food.

   学生たちは、食を通じて環境のために**彼らができること**についてプレゼンテーションを行いました。

3. I made a delicious soup by _____

   _____.

   私は、**卵と冷蔵庫にある材料を組み合わせる**ことで美味しいスープを作りました。

4. The company taught children _____

   _____.

   その会社は、**問題を解決しようと努力する大切さ**を子どもたちに教えました。

B 日清食品について自分の意見を書いてみましょう。

What's your view on NISSIN FOODS Group?

I think NISSIN FOODS Group is a/an _____ group

because _____.

カップヌードルの文字の大きさ

　1966年、安藤百福氏が欧米視察した際、「チキンラーメン」を紙コップに入れお湯を注いでフォークで食べ始めるスーパー担当者の姿を目にしました。百福氏はここから構想を得て、箸とどんぶりを使用しない食習慣の異なる人々でも食べられる「カップヌードル」の開発に取りかかったのです。

　日本で発売されているカップヌードルの商品パッケージには「カップヌードル」とカタカナでも商品名が記載されています。よく見ると「カップヌードル」の「ド」の文字だけ他の文字よりも小さく書かれています。1971年の発売当初、「カップヌードル」という言葉はもちろん、「ヌードル」（noodle）という英語も一般的ではありませんでした。そのため、英語の発音に近づけるために「ド」の文字を小さく表記したのです。

カップヌードルの「ド」の文字が小さく書かれたもう一つの理由は？

a. デザイン性を高めるため
b. 「プードル」と間違えないように
c. 「ヌード」を連想させないように

Unit 4

McDonald's

子どもと家族をハッピーに

Small Chat

右の語句を参考に、次の問いに答えましょう。

> What's your favorite fast food to eat?

> 1.

> Where would you like to work part-time?

> 2.

> What do you keep in mind for traffic safety?

> 3.

| at a convenience store |

| hamburgers |

| wear a helmet |

| fried chicken |

| at a restaurant |

| don't text while walking |

Words and Phrases

 DL 026　◎ CD1-26

A 次の日本語に合う英語を（　　）内に書き入れましょう。

1. 多国籍の　　　　　(m _ _ _ _ _ _ _ _ _ _ _ _ _)

2. 県　　　　　　　 (p _ _ _ _ _ _ _ _ _)

3. 安全　　　　　　 (s _ _ _ _ _)

4. 幼稚園、保育園　 (p _ _ _ _ _ _ _ _)

5. 〜を避ける　　　 (a _ _ _ _)

6. 〜を寄付する　　 (d _ _ _ _ _)

7. 宿泊施設　　　　 (a _ _ _ _ _ _ _ _ _ _ _ _)

8. 洗濯　　　　　　 (l _ _ _ _ _ _)

9. 〜を運営する　　 (m _ _ _ _ _)

10. 費用が高くない　 (i _ _ _ _ _ _ _ _ _ _ _)

B 次の語句に合う日本語訳を選択肢から選びましょう。

1. in total （   ）　　　**a.** 困っている
2. play a role （   ）　　　**b.** 役割を演じる
3. be in trouble （   ）　　　**c.** 募金箱
4. donation box （   ）　　　**d.** お金を集める
5. raise money （   ）　　　**e.** 合計で

Dictation

🎧 DL 027　　💿 CD1-27

音声を聞いて空所を埋めましょう。その後、英文を日本語に訳しましょう。

1. The fast food restaurant is a (　　　　　　　　　　) company.

   _____

2. There is a (　　　　　　) room in the (　　　　　　　　　　).

   _____

3. They will (　　　　) (　　　　　　) to protect children's (　　　　).

   _____

Pre-knowledge

マクドナルドについて調べ、次の1～3が正しければT、間違っていればFを選びましょう。調べた際に、新たに知ったことがあればメモ欄に書き留めましょう。

1. McDonald's started providing security whistles for children's safety in 2020.

   [T / F]

2. McDonald's collects the used toys of the kid's menu for recycling.　　[T / F]

3. The first Ronald McDonald House was built in Philadelphia in 1974.　[T / F]

Speed Reading

次の英文はA～Cの3段落に分かれています。以下のステップに沿って進めましょう。

STEP1 英文を読み、段落ごとにタイムを計りましょう。読むのにかかった時間とWPM（1分あたりに読める語数）を右の **Speed Records** に記録しましょう。

STEP2 英文を再度読みましょう。段落を読み終えるごとに、右の問いに答えましょう。

A 53 words 🎧 DL 028 ◎ CD1-28

McDonald's is a multinational fast food restaurant chain. In Japan, the first restaurant opened in Ginza, Tokyo in 1971. Currently, there are McDonald's restaurants in every prefecture, with about 3,000 restaurants in total. McDonald's makes a great effort to help children grow healthily in body and mind so that
5 families can keep smiling.

B 81 words 🎧 DL 029 ◎ CD1-29

McDonald's popular character, Ronald, plays an important role in a children's safety program. In the "Hello, Ronald!" program, Ronald visits preschools and elementary schools to give lessons about security and traffic rules. Ronald teaches children in a fun, child-friendly way how to protect themselves and avoid
10 dangerous situations. Also, McDonald's contributes to children's safety by donating security whistles to children and providing McDonald's restaurants as a safe place for children to run to if they are in trouble and need help.

C 104 words 🎧 DL 030 ◎ CD1-30

Ronald McDonald's House Charities Japan runs the Ronald McDonald House, which provides accommodations for families who need a place to stay while
15 their child is in the hospital. Based on the concept "Home-away-from-home," the accommodations have a kitchen, living room, laundry room, play room, and a private bedroom so that the families can live comfortably near the hospital. The accommodations are managed by volunteers and available at an inexpensive rate. You can find 12 Ronald McDonald Houses in Japan, and 383 in 45 countries
20 around the world. McDonald's restaurants set a donation box at the counter to raise money to help support these families.

Speed Records

A	53 （語数）÷ _____ （かかった秒数）× **60** （1分あたり）= _____ wpm
B	81 （語数）÷ _____ （かかった秒数）× **60** （1分あたり）= _____ wpm
C	104 （語数）÷ _____ （かかった秒数）× **60** （1分あたり）= _____ wpm

A

1. 日本で最初のマクドナルドはどこにオープンしましたか。 （　　　　　　　）

2. マクドナルドの店舗は世界の約3,000の町にありますか。 （はい・いいえ）

3. マクドナルドが力を注いでいることは何ですか。

   a. 家族と子どもの関係を良くすること　　**b.** 子どもの心身の健康を応援すること

B

1. ドナルドは幼稚園や保育園、小学校を訪れ、防犯や（　　　　　　　）について教え
   ています。　　　　　　　　　　　　　　　　※ドナルドはRonaldの日本での呼び名。

2. ドナルドは子どもたちに（　　　　　　　　　）方法と（　　　　　　　　　）
   方法を教えています。

3. マクドナルドは子どもたちに安全笛を（　　　　　　　）し、子どもたちが困っている
   ときや（　　　　　　　　　）ときに駆け込める場所として店舗を提供しています。

C

1. McDonald's helps families find the most comfortable hospitals. **[T / F]**

2. The Ronald McDonald House helps volunteers save money. **[T / F]**

3. Customers can donate to the Ronald McDonald House at the restaurants.

[T / F]

Dialog

A 次の会話を聞き、空所にあてはまる語を書き入れましょう。　🎧 DL 031　💿 CD1-31

Kento: I like McDonald's good atmosphere. I feel relaxed here and the crews are all nice and ¹·(　　　　　　　).

Emma: I agree. Hey, did you know McDonald's has a Hamburger University? There are only eight universities in total globally, and one of them is in Japan.

Kento: I didn't know that. Hamburger University? What do they study there? Do they study ²·(　　　) ³·(　　　　) make hamburgers?

Emma: McDonald's employees learn leadership and ⁴·(　　　　　　　　　) skills to make restaurants much better in the future.

Kento: Wow, they don't just serve delicious hamburgers. They try to ⁵·(　　　　　　　) the company and play a big role in it.

Emma: That's why McDonald's is ⁶·(　　　　　　) all around the world.

B 次の１〜５のステップで、会話の発話練習をしましょう。

| STEP 1 | 音読し、発音が分からない単語に下線を引きましょう。

| STEP 2 | **A** の音声をもう一度聞いて、発音を確認しましょう。

| STEP 3 | ペアを組み、KentoとEmmaになって読んでみましょう。

| STEP 4 | Kentoのみの音声（🎧 DL 032　💿 CD1-32）を聞き、音声のスピードを意識しながらEmmaのパートを発話しましょう。

| STEP 5 | Emmaのみの音声（🎧 DL 033　💿 CD1-33）を聞き、音声のスピードを意識しながらKentoのパートを発話しましょう。

Expression

A 日本語訳を参考に、英文を完成させましょう。

1. The company contributes to children's education by ＿＿＿＿＿＿＿＿＿ books.
その会社は本**を寄付することで**、子どもたちの教育に貢献しています。

2. The summer festival ＿＿＿＿＿＿＿＿＿＿＿＿＿＿＿ by volunteers last year.
昨年、その夏祭りはボランティアの人たちによって**運営されました**。

3. We set a ＿＿＿＿＿＿＿＿＿＿＿＿＿＿＿＿＿ to help people in trouble.
私たちは困っている人々を助けるため、**お金を集めるために募金箱**を置きました。

4. My sister ＿＿＿＿＿＿＿＿＿＿＿＿＿＿＿＿＿.
私の姉は**そのプログラムで重要な役割を演じています**。

B マクドナルドについて自分の意見を書いてみましょう。

What's your view on McDonald's?

I think McDonald's is a/an ＿＿＿＿＿＿＿＿＿＿＿＿＿ company
because ＿＿＿＿＿＿＿＿＿＿＿＿＿＿＿＿＿＿＿.

Mの由来は？

　英語表記の「McDonald's」の名称ですが、「's」のあとに続くhouseやrestaurantなどの建物を表す名詞が省略されています。これは英語圏でよくある店名の形式です。〈創業者名＋'s〉で「〇〇さんのお店」を表すので、「McDonald's」は創業者の「マクドナルドのお店」といった意味になります。
　ところで、そのマクドナルドのロゴの由来を知っていますか？　有名なマクドナルドのロゴである黄色のMの文字は、McDonald'sの頭文字のMを表していると思うかもしれませんが、実は違います。このロゴが生まれた理由は、イリノイ州のマクドナルド1号店と関係があるのです。

マクドナルドのロゴに使われているMの由来は何でしょう？

a. 1号店店長のイニシャル
b. 1号店店舗のデザイン
c. 1号店店内の落書き

Unit 5

TOYOTA
未来の当たり前を創る Woven City

Small Chat

右の語句を参考に、次の問いに答えましょう。

Do you have a driver's license?

1.

What color car would you like to have?

2.

What function do you expect future cars to have?

3.

black

the ability to fly

red

Yes, I do.

automated driving

No, but I want one.

Words and Phrases
 🎧 DL 034　◎ CD1-34

A 次の日本語に合う英語を（　　）内に書き入れましょう。

1. 〜を設立する　　　　　　(f _ _ _ _)

2. （織物を）織ること、製織　(w _ _ _ _ _ _ _)

3. 重荷　　　　　　　　　　(b _ _ _ _ _)

4. 今日の　　　　　　　　　(p _ _ _ _ _ _ - _ _ _)

5. 具体的な　　　　　　　　(s _ _ _ _ _ _ _)

6. 可能性　　　　　　　　　(p _ _ _ _ _ _ _ _ _ _)

7. 発明家　　　　　　　　　(i _ _ _ _ _ _ _)

8. 〜を奨励する　　　　　　(e _ _ _ _ _ _ _ _)

9. 住人　　　　　　　　　　(r _ _ _ _ _ _ _)

10. 考え　　　　　　　　　　(t _ _ _ _ _ _)

B 次の語句に合う日本語訳を選択肢から選びましょう。

1. vehicle department （　　） **a.** ～に関わっている

2. hand A down to B （　　） **b.** 自動車部門

3. regard A as B （　　） **c.** そのような

4. be involved with ～ （　　） **d.** AをBと見なす

5. like that （　　） **e.** AをBに引き継ぐ

Dictation

DL 035　CD1-35

音声を聞いて空所を埋めましょう。その後、英文を日本語に訳しましょう。

1. The company was (　　　　　　　) in 1926.

_____

2. They are all (　　　　　　) (　　　) (　　　　　　　).

_____

3. Everyone (　　　　　　) (　　　　　　　　　) and tries to create new

(　　　　　　　).

_____

Pre-knowledge

トヨタについて調べ、次の1～3が正しければT、間違っていればFを選びましょう。
調べた際に、新たに知ったことがあればメモ欄に書き留めましょう。

1. Sakichi Toyoda invented an automated weaving machine to help his father.

[T / F]

2. Toyota started to build Woven City in 2007.

[T / F]

3. You can see Mt. Fuji from Woven City.

[T / F]

Speed Reading

次の英文はA〜Cの3段落に分かれています。以下のステップに沿って進めましょう。

STEP 1 英文を読み、段落ごとにタイムを計りましょう。読むのにかかった時間とWPM（1分あたりに読める語数）を右の **Speed Records** に記録しましょう。

STEP 2 英文を再度読みましょう。段落を読み終えるごとに、右の問いに答えましょう。

A **62 words** 🎧 DL 036 ◎ CD1-36

Toyota began as the vehicle department of the Toyota Industries Corporation, founded in 1926. The founder, Sakichi Toyoda, invented the automated weaving machine to reduce his mother's burden during weaving. He always wanted to do good things for others. His idea has been handed down to the present-day Toyota.
5 Now, Toyota is trying to build a test city called the "Woven City."

B **86 words** 🎧 DL 037 ◎ CD1-37

The Woven City is in Susono, Shizuoka Prefecture, where you can see Mt. Fuji. That was the location of Toyota's automobile factories. Now, Toyota plans to develop a new test city there. They have two specific ideas for this project. One is "expanding mobility." Toyota hopes to increase what "mobility" can do for people by
10 connecting that idea with new possibilities. Secondly, Toyota regards every single person involved with this city as an "inventor" and encourages them to invent new services and technologies for the future.

C **109 words** 🎧 DL 038 ◎ CD1-38

When you hear the word "inventor," you may think of a great person very different from you. However, it is not like that. All people in Woven City, such as
15 workers, residents, visitors, kids, and older people, are inventors. Toyota values its motto, "For others," and would like people in Woven City to think of new ideas to improve everyone's life. Inventors will share their thoughts and try them in the Woven City when they find something inconvenient or something they can change for the better. The Woven City is like a test course for new ideas, and Toyota hopes
20 that these ideas will lead to well-being for all.

Speed Records

A 62 (語数) ÷ _____ (かかった秒数) × 60 (1分あたり) = _____ wpm

B 86 (語数) ÷ _____ (かかった秒数) × 60 (1分あたり) = _____ wpm

C 109 (語数) ÷ _____ (かかった秒数) × 60 (1分あたり) = _____ wpm

A

1. トヨタは豊田自動織機の何部門として始まりましたか。 （　　　　　　　）

2. 豊田佐吉が発明したのはどちらですか。
   a. 自動車　　**b.** 自動織機

3. 今のトヨタは豊田佐吉の考え方を継承していますか。 （はい・いいえ）

B

1. ウーブンシティは（　　　　　　　）県（　　　　　　　）市にあります。

2. ウーブンシティプロジェクトの主な考えの1つはモビリティを（　　　　　　　）こ
   とです。

3. トヨタはこの街に関わるすべての人を（　　　　　　　）と見なし、将来のサービス
   や技術を（　　　　　　）することを奨励しています。

C

1. Inventors are always very special and unique people. **[T / F]**

2. In Woven City, children are also encouraged to share ideas. **[T / F]**

3. The people of the city work alone when they want to change something. **[T / F]**

Dialog

A 次の会話を聞き、空所にあてはまる語を書き入れましょう。　　🎧 DL 039　💿 CD1-39

Kento: I'm excited to hear about a city being built for ^{1.}(　　　　　　　) innovation.

Emma: A city built for innovation?

Kento: Yeah, we will see ^{2.}(　　　　) ^{3.}(　　　　) city in Japan!

Emma: Wow! I didn't know that. That's great. Where can we see it?

Kento: At the ^{4.}(　　　　) of Mt. Fuji. Toyota has been developing it. I'm thrilled that new, innovative services may be invented in this city for a better society.

Emma: There seems to be a lot of possibilities in this project, but I can't really imagine what it will be ^{5.}(　　　　).

Kento: That's why it's ^{6.}(　　　　　　). I want to go there when Toyota starts demonstrations.

B 次の1〜5のステップで、会話の発話練習をしましょう。

STEP 1〉 音読し、発音が分からない単語に下線を引きましょう。

STEP 2〉 **A** の音声をもう一度聞いて、発音を確認しましょう。

STEP 3〉 ペアを組み、KentoとEmmaになって読んでみましょう。

STEP 4〉 Kentoのみの音声（🎧 DL 040　💿 CD1-40）を聞き、音声のスピードを意識しながらEmmaのパートを発話しましょう。

STEP 5〉 Emmaのみの音声（🎧 DL 041　💿 CD1-41）を聞き、音声のスピードを意識しながらKentoのパートを発話しましょう。

Expression

A 日本語訳を参考に、英文を完成させましょう。

1. The president's ideas are _____ our staff.
   その社長の考えはスタッフ**に引き継がれています**。

2. The _____ have _____ for improving their town.
   その**住人たちは**、町を良くするための**具体的な考え**を持っています。

3. Toyota's new city _____.
   トヨタの新しい街は**そんな感じではありません**。

4. I _____ that project.
   私はあのプロジェクト**に関わりたいです**。

B トヨタについて自分の意見を書いてみましょう。

What's your view on Toyota?

I think Toyota is a/an _____ company

because _____.

Woven Cityの名に込められた想い

　創業者である豊田佐吉氏の名前は「とよださきち」で、「とよた」ではありません。2022年まで社長だった豊田章男氏ももちろん「とよだあきお」です。トヨタの初期のエンブレムは「TOYODA」でした。ところが、1930年代半ばに、濁点がなくさわやかなこと、8画となり縁起が良いこと、創業者の名字から離れることで個人の会社から社会的な会社へ発展できるという理由から「トヨタ」に変えられました。

　豊田佐吉氏は自動織機を開発しましたが、Woven Cityの名は

weaveの過去分詞形woven「織られた」に由来します。Woven Cityの道は、糸を紡ぐように縦横の道が折り重なります。「自分以外の誰かのために」という佐吉氏から繋がる精神を、この実証実験の街でも引き継いでいく想いが込められています。

トヨタが公開している「クルマまわりの百科事典」より問題です。車関連の英語として通用するのは？

a. ハンドル
b. ワイパー
c. クラクション

STARBUCKS

コーヒーの豆かすを肥料に

Small Chat

右の語句を参考に、次の問いに答えましょう。

How often do you go to a coffee shop?

1.

What do you usually order there?

2.

Have you ever used a paper straw?

3.

once a week

donuts

hot coffee

twice a month

Of course!

Not yet.

Words and Phrases

 DL 042   CD1-42

A 次の日本語に合う英語を（   ）内に書き入れましょう。

1. 貢献する　　　　　(**c** _ _ _ _ _ _ _ _ _)

2. 資源　　　　　　　(**r** _ _ _ _ _ _ _)

3. 施設　　　　　　　(**f** _ _ _ _ _ _ _)

4. 材料　　　　　　　(**i** _ _ _ _ _ _ _ _ _)

5. 〜を減少させる　　(**r** _ _ _ _ _)

6. 排出　　　　　　　(**e** _ _ _ _ _ _ _)

7. 国内の　　　　　　(**d** _ _ _ _ _ _ _)

8. 輸入する　　　　　(**i** _ _ _ _ _)

9. 〜を妨げる　　　　(**p** _ _ _ _ _ _)

10. 使い捨ての　　　　(**d** _ _ _ _ _ _ _ _ _)

B 次の語句に合う日本語訳を選択肢から選びましょう。

1. pay attention to ~ （　　） **a.** 地元の材料

2. sustainable society （　　） **b.** 環境にやさしい社会

3. eco-friendly society （　　） **c.** 持続可能な社会

4. local material （　　） **d.** ～に注意を払う

5. environmental problem （　　） **e.** 環境問題

Dictation

🎧 DL 043　⭕CD1-43

音声を聞いて空所を埋めましょう。その後、英文を日本語に訳しましょう。

1. This store encourages customers not to use (　　　　　　　　) cups.

   _____

2. Young people (　　　) (　　　　　　) (　　　　) creating a sustainable

   society.

   _____

3. How can we (　　　　) CO_2 (　　　　　　) in our daily lives?

   _____

Pre-knowledge

スターバックスについて調べ、次の１～３が正しければT、間違っていればFを選びましょう。調べた際に、新たに知ったことがあればメモ欄に書き留めましょう。

1. Starbucks recycles their coffee grounds into fertilizer. [T / F]

2. Starbucks only uses imported wood for their stores. [T / F]

3. Starbucks stores that are certified for their eco-friendliness are called "Greener
   Stores." [T / F]

Speed Reading

次の英文はA〜Cの3段落に分かれています。以下のステップに沿って進めましょう。

STEP 1 英文を読み、段落ごとにタイムを計りましょう。読むのにかかった時間とWPM（1分あたりに読める語数）を右の **Speed Records** に記録しましょう。

STEP 2 英文を再度読みましょう。段落を読み終えるごとに、右の問いに答えましょう。

A **58 words** 🎧 DL 044 ◎ CD1-44

In 1971, the first Starbucks was built in Seattle, Washington. It quickly became popular. The number of stores has grown to more than 34,000 stores worldwide. This company pays great attention to contributing to people, society, the global environment, and the local community. In order to help build a
5 sustainable society, Starbucks works hard to support various projects.

B **84 words** 🎧 DL 045 ◎ CD1-45

As an environmental project, Starbucks in Japan recycles coffee grounds. Starbucks workers, who are called "partners," turn the waste which is produced after making coffee into a useful resource. They collect the coffee waste and take it to recycling facilities, where it is recycled and turned into compost and animal
10 feed. That compost and feed are used for growing vegetables and feeding cows. The vegetables and the milk of those cows become ingredients for the drinks and food at some Starbucks stores in Japan.

C **115 words** 🎧 DL 046 ◎ CD1-46

Starbucks tries to contribute to an eco-friendly society in many ways. It hopes to reduce CO_2 emissions by 50% by 2030. Some Starbucks stores are trying to use
15 domestic wood rather than imported wood for the materials at their stores. This is because shipping the imported wood produces more CO_2. Also, by making its stores and furniture with local materials, it supports the local industries. This prevents extra environmental problems and also contributes to the domestic forest industry. At a store in Tokyo, which was the first business in Japan to get the
20 "Greener Stores Framework" international certification, it recommends reusable cups to the customers so that it can reduce 75% of their disposable cups.

Speed Records

A 58 （語数）÷ _____ （かかった秒数）× **60** （1分あたり）= _____ wpm

B 84 （語数）÷ _____ （かかった秒数）× **60** （1分あたり）= _____ wpm

C 115 （語数）÷ _____ （かかった秒数）× **60** （1分あたり）= _____ wpm

A

1. スターバックスの1店舗目がオープンしたのはアメリカの何州ですか。

（　　　　　　　　）

2. スターバックスの店舗数は世界に3万店舗以上ありますか。 （ はい・いいえ ）

3. スターバックスは何に貢献することに注意を払っていますか。

a. 人、社会、地球環境、地域社会　　**b.** 人、社会、地球環境、教育

B

1. スターバックスは（　　　　　　　　）のかすをリサイクルしています。

2. 再利用されるかすは（　　　　　　）を育てるため、または

（　　　　　　　　）の餌として使われます。

3. リサイクルによって産出されたものは日本の店舗で（　　　　　　）や

（　　　　　　　）の材料として使われます。

C

1. Starbucks aims to maintain the amount of CO_2 emissions. 　　**[T / F]**

2. Starbucks prefers domestic materials for their stores. 　　**[T / F]**

3. Starbucks encourages customers to use disposable cups. 　　**[T / F]**

Dialog

A 次の会話を聞き、空所にあてはまる語を書き入れましょう。　🎧 DL 047　◎ CD1-47

Kento: It's so ¹·(　　　　　　　　　　　) to have a nice cup of coffee at Starbucks.
Today's English class was enjoyable, but I'm a bit tired because it was hard
to understand.

Emma: Yes, it was. Also, we have to give a presentation about an
²·(　　　　　　　　　　　) society next week!

Kento: We must find a good topic for our presentation.

Emma: Hey, look! The straws are new! These are paper straws, aren't they?

Kento: That's right. I heard that Starbucks is making an ³·(　　　　　　) to build a
⁴·(　　　　　　　　　) society.

Emma: Wow, that's so cool! When I use a paper straw, it makes me feel good that
I'm ⁵·(　　　　　　　　　) ⁶·(　　　　) helping the environment. This
should be our topic for the presentation!

B 次の１〜５のステップで、会話の発話練習をしましょう。

STEP 1 音読し、発音が分からない単語に下線を引きましょう。

STEP 2 **A** の音声をもう一度聞いて、発音を確認しましょう。

STEP 3 ペアを組み、Kentoと Emmaになって読んでみましょう。

STEP 4 Kentoのみの音声（🎧 DL 048　◎ CD1-48 ）を聞き、音声のスピードを意識しながらEmmaのパートを発話しましょう。

STEP 5 Emmaのみの音声（🎧 DL 049　◎ CD1-49 ）を聞き、音声のスピードを意識しながらKentoのパートを発話しましょう。

Expression

A 日本語訳を参考に、英文を完成させましょう。

1. Spending time at Starbucks is _____.
   スターバックスで過ごす時間は**リラックスできます**。

2. Did you know our university uses _____ to make an ecofriendly atmosphere?
   私たちの大学では、環境にやさしい雰囲気を作るために**地元の材料**を使っていることを知っていましたか。

3. Starbucks _____.
   スターバックスは、**環境問題に注意を払っています**。

4. The company _____
   CO₂ emissions.
   その会社は二酸化炭素排出**を減少させるために多大な努力をしています**。

B スターバックスについて自分の意見を書いてみましょう。

What's your view on Starbucks?

I think Starbucks is a/an _____ company

because _____.

スターバックスのロゴ「サイレン」

スターバックスのロゴに描かれている女性は、ギリシャ神話に登場する人魚「サイレン」です。

スターバックスを創業したメンバーの一人が、ノルウェーの木版画に描かれているサイレンを見つけ、ロゴに採用したといわれています。サイレンの美しい歌声が船乗りたちの心を惹きつけるように、多くのお客を魅了したいという想いが込められています。

このロゴに描かれるサイレンの顔は、敢えて左右非対称に描かれています。対称的に作られる工業デザインではなく、人間らしい姿を描くことで親しみを感じてもらえるように、左右のバランスを細部まで計算してデザインしているのです。

2011年にロゴから社名の文字がなくなりました。その理由は？

a. 人魚を目立たせるため
b. 多角的かつ柔軟に事業展開をしていきたいため
c. 企業の認知度が上がって社名を含めなくてよいと判断したため

Unit 7

AEON

豊かな社会を目指した植樹活動

Small Chat

右の語句を参考に、次の問いに答えましょう。

What do you usually do at shopping malls?

> 1.

Have you ever planted anything?

> 2.

What animals or insects do you often see?

> 3.

| flowers |

| watch movies |

| ladybugs |

| vegetables |

| buy snacks |

| crows |

Words and Phrases

 DL 050 CD1-50

A 次の日本語に合う英語を（　　）内に書き入れましょう。

1. 数字　　　　　　　　（ f _ _ _ _ _ ）

2. 小売り業　　　　　　（ r _ _ _ _ _ _ _ _ ）

3. 〜を表す　　　　　　（ r _ _ _ _ _ _ _ _ ）

4. 〜を植える　　　　　（ p _ _ _ _ ）

5. 花が咲く　　　　　　（ b _ _ _ ）

6. 〜するときはいつでも（ w _ _ _ _ _ _ _ ）

7. 〜を維持する　　　　（ m _ _ _ _ _ _ ）

8. 生物多様性　　　　　（ b _ _ _ _ _ _ _ _ _ _ _ ）

9. 昆虫　　　　　　　　（ b _ _ ）

10. 生息地　　　　　　　（ h _ _ _ _ _ ）

B 次の語句に合う日本語訳を選択肢から選びましょう。

1. the number of ~   (   )   **a.** さまざまな生き物

2. a source of ~   (   )   **b.** ～の源

3. various creatures   (   )   **c.** ～の量

4. CO_2 absorption   (   )   **d.** 二酸化炭素吸収

5. amount of ~   (   )   **e.** ～の数

Dictation

🎧 DL 051   ◎ CD1-51

音声を聞いて空所を埋めましょう。その後、英文を日本語に訳しましょう。

1. The town is planning to increase the (   ) of trees from April.

   _____

2. Nature can be (   ) (   ) (   ) happiness.

   _____

3. (   ) refers to all living creatures, from bugs to humans.

   _____

Pre-knowledge

イオンについて調べ、次の 1 ～ 3 が正しければT、間違っていればFを選びましょう。
調べた際に、新たに知ったことがあればメモ欄に書き留めましょう。

1. Aeon started a project to plant trees in 2000.   [T / F]

2. Aeon has been planting trees only domestically.   [T / F]

3. People have chances to observe nature at Aeon.   [T / F]

Speed Reading

次の英文はA～Cの3段落に分かれています。以下のステップに沿って進めましょう。

STEP 1 英文を読み、段落ごとにタイムを計りましょう。読むのにかかった時間とWPM（1分あたりに読める語数）を右の**Speed Records**に記録しましょう。

STEP 2 英文を再度読みましょう。段落を読み終えるごとに、右の問いに答えましょう。

A **61 words** 🎧 DL 052 ◎ CD1-52

12,554,305. Can you guess what this figure means for Aeon? You may think it is the number of employees or products because Aeon is a leading retailing and shopping mall business in Japan. However, this figure represents the number of trees Aeon has planted. Aeon started planting in 1991 in order to help solve
5　environmental problems and achieve a peaceful society.

B **78 words** 🎧 DL 053 ◎ CD1-53

One day, a president of Aeon found that the trees in his garden did not bloom. He realized that the more the economy grew, the dirtier the sky got, and that losing nature meant losing a source of abundance. Thus, Aeon began to plant trees with local people whenever it built a new store. It was the start of the Aeon
10　Hometown Forests Program. After 30 years, more than one thousand stores have forests where various creatures live.

C **107 words** 🎧 DL 054 ◎ CD1-54

Recently, companies have been focused on maintaining biodiversity. Supporting biodiversity means keeping all creatures on earth, from bugs to humans, together in a healthy balance. Aeon knows the environmental value of their forests, from the
15　amount of CO_2 absorption to its role in biodiversity through providing habitats for birds, insects, and plants. As a result, Aeon can contribute to society by increasing biodiversity and creating beautiful natural spaces. Neighborhood children can enjoy this, too. It is a good chance for them to observe and touch nature. Now, Aeon is aiming to reach a goal of another ten million trees with help from people of the
20　local community.

Speed Records

A　61（語数）÷ _____（かかった秒数）× **60**（1分あたり）= _____ wpm

B　78（語数）÷ _____（かかった秒数）× **60**（1分あたり）= _____ wpm

C　107（語数）÷ _____（かかった秒数）× **60**（1分あたり）= _____ wpm

A

1. イオンはこれまでに何本の木を植えましたか。　　　　　（　　　　　　　　）

2. イオンが日本で牽引しているのはショッピングモール事業と何ですか。

（　　　　　　　　　）

3. イオンが植樹をする目的は環境問題の解決と何ですか。
a. 平和な社会の実現　　　**b.** 公平な社会の実現

B

1. ある日、イオンの社長は庭の木の花が（　　　　　　　　）ことに気づきました。

2. イオンの社長は自然を失うことは、（　　　　　　　　）を失うと考えました。

3. 植樹を始めて30年が経ち、森のあるイオンは全国で（　　　　　　　）店舗以上となり、森には（　　　　　　　　　）が棲んでいます。

C

1. Biodiversity means various creatures living together in harmony.　**[T / F]**

2. The main purpose of creating natural spaces is that they can be places for kids to play.　**[T / F]**

3. Aeon aims to continue planting another 10 million trees.　**[T / F]**

Dialog

A 次の会話を聞き、空所にあてはまる語を書き入れましょう。　🎧 DL 055　💿 CD1-55

Kento: Listen, I participated in a nature observation event at my younger sister's school yesterday.

Emma: Oh, that's nice. Did you go to a mountain or a river? Did you see any
1·(　　　　　　)? Were the flowers 2·(　　　　　　　)?

Kento: Actually, I went to the Aeon over there.

Emma: Aeon? What do you 3·(　　　　) by that?

Kento: You know, there's a forest area near the gate of the mall. You can see
4·(　　　　　) 5·(　　　　　　　) and a little river there. My sister was so excited to see a wild frog.

Emma: That sounds great! It's nice to know that there's a relaxing place to
6·(　　　) by whenever I want. I'll go tomorrow!

B 次の１〜５のステップで、会話の発話練習をしましょう。

STEP 1〉 音読し、発音が分からない単語に下線を引きましょう。

STEP 2〉 **A**の音声をもう一度聞いて、発音を確認しましょう。

STEP 3〉 ペアを組み、KentoとEmmaになって読んでみましょう。

STEP 4〉 Kentoのみの音声（🎧 DL 056　💿 CD1-56 ）を聞き、音声のスピードを意識しながらEmmaのパートを発話しましょう。

STEP 5〉 Emmaのみの音声（🎧 DL 057　💿 CD1-57 ）を聞き、音声のスピードを意識しながらKentoのパートを発話しましょう。

Expression

A 日本語訳を参考に、英文を完成させましょう。

1. Forests protect the habitats of _____.
森は**さまざまな生き物**の生息地を保護しています。

2. Cherry blossoms _____ in May in Hokkaido.
北海道では、桜が5月に**咲き始めます**。

3. The figure _____ in this forest.
その数字はこの森の**鳥の数**を表しています。

4. Can you guess _____ ?
生物多様性が何を意味するか、あなたは推測できますか。

B イオンについて自分の意見を書いてみましょう。

What's your view on Aeon?

I think Aeon is a/an _____ company

because _____ .

「大黒柱に車をつけよ」

　イオンの始まりは1700年代にさかのぼります。初代岡田惣左衛門が太物・小間物商を三重県四日市で創業しました。岡田屋の家訓の一つに「大黒柱に車をつけよ」というものがありました。「大黒柱に車」、すぐに理解するのが難しい言葉ですね。これは「発展性の高い場所があれば、迷わずに店を移す」という意味で、お客や社会の流れに合わせて柔軟に変化していく必要性を示しています。この家訓の精神が今のイオンにも流れています。AEONの由来は、ラテン語で「永遠」を表す「アイオーン」です。「夢のある未来」という意味を付加し「私たち自身が夢の未来を作る担い手になる」という意思を込めているそうです。

イオンのロゴのEとOをつなぐリングは、何という名前でしょう？

a. アースリング
b. マリッジリング
c. エターナルリング

Unit 8

NIKE

誰もが運動を楽しめる社会に

Small Chat

右の語句を参考に、次の問いに答えましょう。

> What is your favorite sport to play?

1.

> How often do you play sports?

2.

> What do you think the benefits of physical activity are?

3.

| better health |
| tennis |
| every day |
| less stress |
| once a week |
| soccer |

Words and Phrases

 🎧 DL 058　💿 CD2-02

A 次の日本語に合う英語を（　　）内に書き入れましょう。

1. 実用的な　　　　　(**p** _ _ _ _ _ _ _ _)

2. 約束、責任　　　　(**c** _ _ _ _ _ _ _ _ _ _)

3. 専門家　　　　　　(**e** _ _ _ _ _ _)

4. 鬼ごっこ　　　　　(**t** _ _)

5. 自主性、独立　　　(**i** _ _ _ _ _ _ _ _ _ _ _)

6. ～をやめる　　　　(**q** _ _ _)

7. ～を育てる　　　　(**f** _ _ _ _ _)

8. ～を耕す、～を養う(**c** _ _ _ _ _ _ _)

9. 可能性、潜在能力　(**p** _ _ _ _ _ _ _ _)

10. ～を追求する　　　(**p** _ _ _ _ _)

B 次の語句に合う日本語訳を選択肢から選びましょう。

1. combine A with B   (   )   **a.** 前進する

2. PE class   (   )   **b.** AだけでなくBも

3. not only A but (also) B   (   )   **c.** 〜に参加する

4. participate in 〜   (   )   **d.** AとBを組み合わせる

5. make steps   (   )   **e.** 体育の授業

Dictation

🎧 DL 059   ◉ CD2-03

音声を聞いて空所を埋めましょう。その後、英文を日本語に訳しましょう。

1. He (   ) sports (   ) music to create a new game.

   _____

2. (   ) (   ) did the girl play tennis, but she also played (   )

   with her friend.

   _____

3. Children can cultivate their (   ) through (   ).

   _____

Pre-knowledge

ナイキについて調べ、次の1〜3が正しければT、間違っていればFを選びましょう。
調べた際に、新たに知ったことがあればメモ欄に書き留めましょう。

1. Nike supports women's participation in sports.   [T / F]

2. Nike's mission is to bring inspiration and innovation to every athlete in the world.   [T / F]

3. Nike's project for a sustainable society is called "Move Together."   [T / F]

Speed Reading

次の英文はA～Cの3段落に分かれています。以下のステップに沿って進めましょう。

STEP 1 英文を読み、段落ごとにタイムを計りましょう。読むのにかかった時間とWPM（1分あたりに読める語数）を右の *Speed Records* に記録しましょう。

STEP 2 英文を再度読みましょう。段落を読み終えるごとに、右の問いに答えましょう。

A **69 words** 🎧 DL 060 ◉ CD2-04

Nike is an American sporting goods company. Their products are popular among young people for fashion as well as for practical use. Nike has made a commitment to get young people, especially kids, moving. The commitment is called "Made to Play," which means "kids are born to move." In order to support children's health and happiness,
5 Nike provides opportunities for children to move and be active through this program.

B **84 words** 🎧 DL 061 ◉ CD2-05

Nike worked with various experts to create the JUMP-JAM program. In this program, there are 80 kinds of unique games which combine sports like throwing balls with playful activities such as tag or rock-paper-scissors. The rules of those games are easy for younger children to understand, and they can be used in PE
10 classes at schools. Through the program, children are not only able to improve their mental and physical health, but also learn independence and increase their social skills by communicating with others.

C **116 words** 🎧 DL 062 ◉ CD2-06

Nike also supports women's participation in sports. It is said that the number of girls under 15 who quit playing sports is double that of boys in Tokyo. Nike set
15 up "Play Academy with Naomi Osaka" in collaboration with tennis athlete Naomi Osaka. To achieve gender equality, this program aims at promoting opportunities for girls to participate in sports and fostering female leaders in sports. Naomi Osaka cooperates with this program in the hope that by playing sports, girls can experience the joy of sports, cultivate their potential, and become good role models
20 for future generations. The field of sports is a perfect place to make steps towards pursuing a society where everyone has equal opportunities.

A

1. ナイキはどんな商品を扱う企業ですか。　　　　　　　　　（　　　　　　　　　）

2. ナイキが掲げる「Made to Play」の意味は何ですか。

   a. 子どもは動くために生まれてきた。　**b.** 子どもは遊びを作り出さなければならない。

3. ナイキは子どもが活動的になる機会を提供していますか。　　　　（はい・いいえ）

B

1. ナイキは（　　　　　　　　　）と共同してスポーツと遊びを（　　　　　　　　　）、80種類の運動を作りました。

2. 運動の（　　　　　　　　　）は幼い子どもにも理解できる簡単なものであり、この運動は（　　　　　　　　　）で活用されています。

3. この運動を通して、子どもたちは、心身の健康状態を良くするだけでなく、（　　　　　　　　　）を学び、（　　　　　　　　　）を身に付けることができます。

C

1. It is more likely for boys to give up playing sports than girls in Tokyo. **[T / F]**

2. An organization collaborated with Nike to set up the "Play Academy." **[T / F]**

3. Nike supports girls to build leadership skills through sports. **[T / F]**

Dialog

A 次の会話を聞き、空所にあてはまる語を書き入れましょう。　🎧 DL 063 　◎ CD2-07

Kento: Emma, your tennis shoes are really cool. I like the color!

Emma: Thank you, Kento. They are my favorite. I'll ¹·( ) in the tennis tournament tomorrow with these shoes!

Kento: That's great! I think you've been playing tennis for more than ten years, right? That's ²·( ). I'm proud of your passion for sports.

Emma: To be honest, I thought about ³·( ) tennis when I was in high school. But I decided to continue to play because playing sports is enjoyable.

Kento: For sure! By the way, I've heard Nike supports women's participation in sports. I hope female ⁴·( ) will be more active in the field of sports.

Emma: I hope so, too. For now, I'll do my best and win first ⁵·( ) tomorrow!

B 次の 1 〜 5 のステップで、会話の発話練習をしましょう。

STEP **1** ▷ 音読し、発音が分からない単語に下線を引きましょう。

STEP **2** ▷ **A** の音声をもう一度聞いて、発音を確認しましょう。

STEP **3** ▷ ペアを組み、KentoとEmmaになって読んでみましょう。

STEP **4** ▷ Kentoのみの音声（🎧 DL 064 　◎ CD2-08 ）を聞き、音声のスピードを意識しながらEmmaのパートを発話しましょう。

STEP **5** ▷ Emmaのみの音声（🎧 DL 065 　◎ CD2-09 ）を聞き、音声のスピードを意識しながらKentoのパートを発話しましょう。

Expression

A 日本語訳を参考に、英文を完成させましょう。

1. Many young people improved their _____ through sports.

   多くの若者がスポーツを通して**精神面の健康**を向上させました。

2. He thought about _____ when he was in high school.

   彼は高校のとき、**野球を辞めること**について考えました。

3. This course aims at promoting opportunities for students to _____ _____ and learn _____.

   この講座は、学生が**スポーツに参加して自主性**を学ぶ機会を推進することを目的としています。

4. To achieve _____

   _____.

   ジェンダー平等を達成するため、**私たちは女性のリーダーを育てるべきです**。

B ナイキについて自分の意見を書いてみましょう。

What's your view on Nike?

Nike is a/an _____ company

because _____.

ナイキのロゴは女神の翼

　シンプルなデザインでありながら勢いが感じられるナイキのロゴ。これは同社の創設者フィル・ナイト氏が、当時まだ学生だったキャロライン・デビッドソン氏に制作を依頼し、1971年に誕生しました。このロゴには「ビューンと音を立てる」の意味があり、躍動感やス

ピード感を表現して「Swoosh（スウッシュ）」という名前が付けられました。ロゴのデザインはギリシャ神話に出てくる女神「ニケ（Nike）」像の翼をモチーフにしています。ニケは英語で「ナイキ」と読み、同社のブランド名もこの女神の名にちなんで付けられました。

Quiz!

ギリシャ神話に登場する女神Nikeは何の女神でしょう？

a. 青春の女神
b. 勝利の女神
c. 運命の女神

MUJI

地域と連携した公園づくり

Small Chat

右の語句を参考に、次の問いに答えましょう。

Do you like shopping alone or with someone?

> 1.

| with friends |

| modern |

What style of furniture do you prefer?

> 2.

| once in a while |

| by myself |

How often do you communicate with your neighbors?

> 3.

| classic |

| Not much. |

Words and Phrases

 DL 066　　CD2-10

A 次の日本語に合う英語を（　　）内に書き入れましょう。

1. 小売り　　　　　　(r _ _ _ _ _)

2. 人気のある　　　　(p _ _ _ _ _ _ _)

3. 地元の、地方の　　(l _ _ _ _)

4. 地域社会　　　　　(c _ _ _ _ _ _ _ _)

5. 心身の健康　　　　(w _ _ _ _ _ _ _)

6. 薬局　　　　　　　(p _ _ _ _ _ _ _)

7. 測定　　　　　　　(m _ _ _ _ _ _ _ _ _ _)

8. ～を活性化する　　(r _ _ _ _ _ _ _ _ _ _)

9. ～を改装する　　　(r _ _ _ _ _ _ _)

10. 既存の　　　　　　(e _ _ _ _ _ _ _)

B 次の語句に合う日本語訳を選択肢から選びましょう。

1. a variety of ~ (   )   **a.** 〜に立ち寄る

2. in association with ~ (   )   **b.** 〜に基づいて

3. stop by ~ (   )   **c.** 気軽に〜する

4. feel free to ~ (   )   **d.** さまざまな〜

5. based on ~ (   )   **e.** 〜と連携して

Dictation

🎧 DL 067   ◎ CD2-11

音声を聞いて空所を埋めましょう。その後、英文を日本語に訳しましょう。

1. Muji's goods are (   ) in many countries.

   _____

2. The company supports the (   ) of the local people.

   _____

3. City officials (   ) the park in (   ) with a

   company.

   _____

Pre-knowledge

無印良品について調べ、次の1〜3が正しければT、間違っていればFを選びましょう。
調べた際に、新たに知ったことがあればメモ欄に書き留めましょう。

1. The first Muji shop opened in Kyoto in 1983.   [T / F]

2. Muji renovated a station waiting room in Miyazaki.   [T / F]

3. Muji formed a partnership with Tokyo's Toshima Ward in 2017.   [T / F]

Speed Reading

次の英文はA～Cの3段落に分かれています。以下のステップに沿って進めましょう。

STEP 1 英文を読み、段落ごとにタイムを計りましょう。読むのにかかった時間と WPM（1分あたりに読める語数）を右の *Speed Records* に記録しましょう。

STEP 2 英文を再度読みましょう。段落を読み終えるごとに、右の問いに答えましょう。

A **65 words** 🎧 DL 068 ◎ CD2-12

Muji was founded in 1980 as a retail store which sells a variety of quality goods such as clothes, food, and household items. Muji's simple but practical goods are popular in many Asian and European countries, the U.S., and, of course, Japan. Not only does Muji sell good products, but it also aims to bring energy to
5 the local community by connecting people with society.

B **86 words** 🎧 DL 069 ◎ CD2-13

One of their efforts involving the local community can be seen in shops in Niigata and Hiroshima. In order to support the wellness and healthy lifestyles of the locals, they opened "a city nurse's office." There, they provide medicines to people in the community as a town pharmacy in association with the hospitals
10 nearby. They also host events, such as health counseling, physical measurement, and exercise classes. Muji provides a place where anyone can stop by and feel free to ask for advice about their health.

C **119 words** 🎧 DL 070 ◎ CD2-14

In addition, Muji worked with city officials in Tokyo to revitalize local parks that were not fully used by families with young children. Based on ideas shared
15 with the local people, they renovated parks while reusing existing facilities. They made "park-trucks" in collaboration with a car company, and drove from one park to another in order to deliver snacks, drinks, or library books to the local people. Also, they created unique park signs, which show "what you can do" instead of "what you cannot do" in the park. This change from negative to positive messages
20 aims to increase what children can enjoy in the park. Perhaps you can see Muji's efforts to improve the local community in your town.

Speed Records

A 65 (語数) ÷ _____ (かかった秒数) × **60** (1分あたり) = _____ wpm

B 86 (語数) ÷ _____ (かかった秒数) × **60** (1分あたり) = _____ wpm

C 119 (語数) ÷ _____ (かかった秒数) × **60** (1分あたり) = _____ wpm

A

1. 無印良品はいつ設立しましたか。　　　　　　　　　　（　　　　　　　　）

2. 無印良品はヨーロッパで人気がありますか。　　　　　（はい・いいえ）

3. 無印良品は、なぜ地域の人々と社会をつなぐ活動をしていますか。
   a. 販売を促進させるため　　**b.** 地域社会を活性化させるため

B

1. 無印良品は地元の人々の健康を支えるために「まちの（　　　　　）」を開設しました。

2. 無印良品は、（　　　　　　）や身体測定、（　　　　　　）などのイベントを開催しています。

3. 無印良品は、誰でも（　　　　　　）ことができ、（　　　　　　）について気軽に相談できる場所の提供を目指しています。

C

1. "Park-trucks" deliver a variety of things, such as food, to the locals.　**[T / F]**

2. The park signs use positive language to support children's enjoyment.　**[T / F]**

3. Muji and a city in Tokyo are collaborating to build new parks overseas.　**[T / F]**

Dialog

A 次の会話を聞き、空所にあてはまる語を書き入れましょう。　🎧 DL 071　◎ CD2-15

Emma:　I like Muji's furniture because it's simple and ¹·(　　　　　).

Kento:　I agree with you. I'm now thinking about buying a study desk there.

Emma:　Oh, sounds good! Speaking of Muji, I heard it helped ²·(　　　　　)
　　　　old residences and station waiting rooms.

Kento:　I've heard that. It remodeled the waiting room of a station in Miyazaki very
　　　　stylishly.

Emma:　It became a nice and ³·(　　　　　　　　) place where high school
　　　　students come to study or the ⁴·(　　　　) people enjoy chatting.

Kento:　Muji's good taste makes places better. I'm sure the desk will
　　　　⁵·(　　　　　) a cozy atmosphere in my room.

B 次の1～5のステップで、会話の発話練習をしましょう。

STEP 1〉音読し、発音が分からない単語に下線を引きましょう。

STEP 2〉**A**の音声をもう一度聞いて、発音を確認しましょう。

STEP 3〉ペアを組み、EmmaとKentoになって読んでみましょう。

STEP 4〉Emmaのみの音声（🎧 DL 072　◎ CD2-16）を聞き、音声のスピードを意識し
　　　　ながらKentoのパートを発話しましょう。

STEP 5〉Kentoのみの音声（🎧 DL 073　◎ CD2-17）を聞き、音声のスピードを意識し
　　　　ながらEmmaのパートを発話しましょう。

Expression

A 日本語訳を参考に、英文を完成させましょう。

1. I enjoy eating _____ dishes.
   私は**さまざまな**料理を食べるのが好きです。

2. Volunteers _____ in the office.
   ボランティアたちはオフィスの**古い設備を新しくしました**。

3. The sign shows _____ in the park.
   その看板は**子どもたちが**公園で**できること**を示しています。

4. The company _____.
   その企業は**地元の地域社会に貢献しています**。

B 無印良品について自分の意見を書いてみましょう。

What's your view on Muji?

I think Muji is a/an _____ brand

because _____.

ラベルの「薄いベージュ色」

　生活に根ざした幅広い製品を取り扱う無印良品は、1980年に株式会社西友のプライベートブランドとして販売をスタートしました。

　「わけあって、安い。」という当時のキャッチコピーのもと、同社は生産プロセスの合理化を進めることで、シンプルな低価格商品の提供を目指しました。例えば、同社のラベルやパッケージ素材に薄いベージュ色が多く使われている理由をご存知ですか？　これは、紙の原料であるパルプを漂白するプロセスを省略したことから用いられ始めました。

　経済成長を遂げ、華美な商品に価値が見出されていた時代に、「印のない」、無駄を排除した同社の品は画期的で、多くの人々に支持されました。

無印良品には環境・社会に配慮した3つの視点があります。「素材の選択」「工程の点検」そして最後の視点は次のどれでしょう？

a. 包装の簡略化
b. 生産の自動化
c. 再利用の徹底

Apple

リサイクルロボット DaisyとDave

Small Chat

右の語句を参考に、次の問いに答えましょう。

How much time do you spend on your phone daily?

1.

What are your favorite apps to use on your phone?

2.

What will you do with your old phone?

3.

about an hour

social media

throw it away

about 2-3 hours

online shopping

sell it

Words and Phrases

 DL 074　CD2-18

A 次の日本語に合う英語を（　　）内に書き入れましょう。

1. 装置　　　　　　　　（ **d** _ _ _ _ _ ）

2. 〜に動力を供給する　（ **p** _ _ _ _ ）

3. 容器　　　　　　　　（ **c** _ _ _ _ _ _ _ _ ）

4. リサイクル可能な　　（ **r** _ _ _ _ _ _ _ _ _ ）

5. 〜を分解する　　　　（ **d** _ _ _ _ _ _ _ _ _ _ ）

6. 〜を完成させる　　　（ **c** _ _ _ _ _ _ _ ）

7. 効率よく　　　　　　（ **e** _ _ _ _ _ _ _ _ _ _ ）

8. 質　　　　　　　　　（ **q** _ _ _ _ _ ）

9. 貴重な　　　　　　　（ **p** _ _ _ _ _ _ _ ）

10. 原料、材料　　　　　（ **m** _ _ _ _ _ _ _ ）

B 次の語句に合う日本語訳を選択肢から選びましょう。

1. global environment （　） **a.** ～を取り出す
2. renewable energy （　） **b.** 天然資源
3. take apart ~ （　） **c.** 再生可能エネルギー
4. take out ~ （　） **d.** ～を分解する
5. natural resource （　） **e.** 地球環境

Dictation

DL 075　CD2-19

音声を聞いて空所を埋めましょう。その後、英文を日本語に訳しましょう。

1. The machine can (　　　　) smartphones into recyclable (　　　　).

2. We have to consider the (　　　) (　　　　　　) for our future.

3. The robot (　　　　) takes out (　　　　) materials.

Pre-knowledge

アップルについて調べ、次の１～３が正しければT、間違っていればFを選びましょう。調べた際に、新たに知ったことがあればメモ欄に書き留めましょう。

1. Apple was founded in 1976 by four people, including Steve Jobs. [T / F]

2. Apple expects that all Apple products will be produced with 100% clean energy by 2030. [T / F]

3. In 2021, nearly 20% of all the materials used in Apple products were recycled materials. [T / F]

Speed Reading

次の英文はA～Cの3段落に分かれています。以下のステップに沿って進めましょう。

STEP 1 英文を読み、段落ごとにタイムを計りましょう。読むのにかかった時間と WPM（1分あたりに読める語数）を右の *Speed Records* に記録しましょう。

STEP 2 英文を再度読みましょう。段落を読み終えるごとに、右の問いに答えましょう。

A **66 words** 🎧 DL 076 ◎ CD2-20

Apple is an American technology company, founded in 1976, that mainly sells digital devices and software. Their functional and stylish products are popular all over the world. Considering not only their users but also the global environment, Apple uses renewable energy to power their whole company. They have announced
5 that they will use recycled materials for all of their products and packaging containers in the future.

B **77 words** 🎧 DL 077 ◎ CD2-21

Apple develops recycling technology to reuse parts of their products. An original recycling robot, Daisy, can disassemble iPhones made from various kinds of metals, such as aluminum, gold, and cobalt, into recyclable materials. It can
10 disassemble 200 iPhones an hour and 1.2 million a year. After Daisy takes apart a variety of materials, another robot, Dave, takes out important material called rare-earth elements. With the latest recycling machine, Taz, the recycling process is completed even more efficiently.

C **101 words** 🎧 DL 078 ◎ CD2-22

Apple's recycling robots take out metals like gold and copper. These metals
15 can be used for new products because of their high quality. From the same weight of parts, recycling robots take 2,000 times more gold and copper from old iPhones than do recycling companies. Thanks to these robots, 59% of all the aluminum used for Apple products in 2021 was collected from recycled materials. In addition, there are many Apple products whose frames and bodies are made of 100%
20 recycled aluminum. By recycling and reusing precious materials, Apple protects the earth's natural resources and places great value on our future.

Speed Records

A 66（語数）÷ _____（かかった秒数）× **60**（1分あたり）= _____ wpm

B 77（語数）÷ _____（かかった秒数）× **60**（1分あたり）= _____ wpm

C 101（語数）÷ _____（かかった秒数）× **60**（1分あたり）= _____ wpm

A

1. アップルが主に販売しているのは、ソフトウエアと何ですか。　（　　　　　　　　　　）

2. アップルは会社全体で使用する電力を再生可能エネルギーでまかなっていますか。

（はい・いいえ）

3. アップルは将来、何にリサイクル素材を使用すると言っていますか。

　　a. すべての店舗看板　　**b.** すべての製品と包装容器

B

1. アップルは、製品を（　　　　　　　　　）するための技術開発に取り組んでいます。

2. デイジーは1時間に（　　　　　　　　）台のiPhoneをリサイクル可能なパーツに（　　　　　　　　）することができます。

3. デイヴは、（　　　　　　　　）が素材を分解した後、重要な素材である（　　　　　　　　）を取り出します。

C

1. Metals like gold and copper are extremely difficult to reuse.　**[T / F]**

2. Over half of the aluminum for Apple items in 2021 was from used parts.　**[T / F]**

3. A lot of Apple products have parts fully made from recycled aluminum.　**[T / F]**

Dialog

A 次の会話を聞き、空所にあてはまる語を書き入れましょう。　🎧 DL 079　💿 CD2-23

Emma: I'm thinking of buying a new smartphone, but my smartphone isn't broken. Do you think it's a ^{1.}(　　　　　） if I buy a new one?

Kento: Um …. I don't know, but I heard that old smartphones are not always ^{2.}(　　　　　） ^{3.}(　　　　　）. Some of them are recycled.

Emma: Really? I wonder how they are recycled.

Kento: For example, if they still work, people resell them as second-hand phones. If they are broken, they are disassembled and recycled as ^{4.}(　　　　　） for new products.

Emma: Oh, I didn't know that. It sounds good because recycling protects natural ^{5.}(　　　　　）. I think there are many other things we can recycle in our daily life.

Kento: You're right. Let's find out what we can do to help the ^{6.}(　　　　　）.

B 次の1～5のステップで、会話の発話練習をしましょう。

STEP 1〉 音読し、発音が分からない単語に下線を引きましょう。

STEP 2〉 **A** の音声をもう一度聞いて、発音を確認しましょう。

STEP 3〉 ペアを組み、EmmaとKentoになって読んでみましょう。

STEP 4〉 Emmaのみの音声（🎧 DL 080　💿 CD2-24 ）を聞き、音声のスピードを意識しながらKentoのパートを発話しましょう。

STEP 5〉 Kentoのみの音声（🎧 DL 081　💿 CD2-25 ）を聞き、音声のスピードを意識しながらEmmaのパートを発話しましょう。

Expression

A 日本語訳を参考に、英文を完成させましょう。

1. This T-shirt _____ recycled plastic bottles.
   このTシャツは再利用されたペットボトル**でできています**。

2. The robot can _____ an hour.
   そのロボットは1時間に**200台のスマートフォンを分解できます**。

3. If smartphones are _____, they _____

   _____ for new products.
   もしスマートフォンが**壊れて**いる場合、それらは新しい製品のための**原料としてリサイクルされます**。

4. I want to _____

   _____.

   私は**世界中の人々におしゃれな製品を紹介し**たいです。

B アップルについて自分の意見を書いてみましょう。

What's your view on Apple?

I think Apple is a/an _____ company

because _____.

シンプルへの道

　アップルの創業者であり、iPhoneの生みの親としても知られるスティーブ・ジョブズ氏。死後10年以上が経過する今もなお、彼の残した功績や言葉は世界中のビジネスマンに影響力を与えています。彼が残した言葉に次のものがあります。

"Simple can be harder than complex."
（シンプルはときに複雑よりも難しいものだ）

　物事をシンプルにするためには、努力をして思考を単純化する必要があり、それができれば山さえも動かす力があると説きました。成長

を遂げる企業は、働く人々も提供するサービスも増え、複雑化していくものです。しかし、徹底的に無駄を排除して洗練さを追求したジョブズ氏の哲学は、同社の製品を通して多くの人の心を動かしています。

りんごのマークで知られるアップルのロゴですが、創業時のロゴはどんなデザインだったでしょう？

a. ニュートンがりんごをかじっているデザイン

b. ニュートンが落ちたりんごを眺めているデザイン

c. ニュートンがりんごの木の下で読書しているデザイン

Unit 11
Rakuten Group
多様性に配慮した働き方

Small Chat

右の語句を参考に、次の問いに答えましょう。

> What country would you like to visit?

> 1.

> What foreign food is your favorite?

> 2.

> When do you use English in your daily life?

> 3.

England

Chinese

in class

Italian

India

with my friends

Words and Phrases

 DL 082  CD2-26

A 次の日本語に合う英語を（　　）内に書き入れましょう。

1. 宗教 　　　　　　　　　　　　(r _ _ _ _ _ _ _)

2. 〜を促進する 　　　　　　　　(f _ _ _ _ _ _ _ _ _ _)

3. 〜を発表する 　　　　　　　　(a _ _ _ _ _ _ _)

4. 〜を採用する、〜を募集する 　(r _ _ _ _ _ _ _)

5. 食堂 　　　　　　　　　　　　(c _ _ _ _ _ _ _ _)

6. 〜を祈る 　　　　　　　　　　(p _ _ _)

7. 雰囲気 　　　　　　　　　　　(a _ _ _ _ _ _ _ _ _)

8. 協働して 　　　　　　　　　　(c _ _ _ _ _ _ _ _ _ _ _ _ _ _ _)

9. 絶対必要な 　　　　　　　　　(e _ _ _ _ _ _ _ _)

10. 〜に力を与える 　　　　　　　(e _ _ _ _ _ _)

68

B 次の語句に合う日本語訳を選択肢から選びましょう。

1. official language 　　　（　　　） 　　**a.** 異文化交流
2. in fact 　　　　　　　　（　　　） 　　**b.** 実際
3. head for ~ 　　　　　　（　　　） 　　**c.** その上
4. what's more 　　　　　（　　　） 　　**d.** 公用語
5. cross-cultural exchange （　　　） 　　**e.** ～に向かう

Dictation

🎧 DL 083 　◎ CD2-27

音声を聞いて空所を埋めましょう。その後、英文を日本語に訳しましょう。

1. People from different nationalities and (　　　　　　　　) can work together.

   _____

2. These companies (　　　　　) (　　　　　　　　) people every year.

   _____

3. We are (　　　　　) (　　　) the same (　　　　).

   _____

Pre-knowledge

楽天について調べ、次の1～3が正しければT、間違っていればFを選びましょう。調べた際に、新たに知ったことがあればメモ欄に書き留めましょう。

1. Rakuten does not work on facilitating diversity at all. 　　[T / F]

2. Rakuten has used English as its official language since 2009. 　　[T / F]

3. Rakuten employees take part in a cross-cultural exchange program. 　　[T / F]

Speed Reading

次の英文はA～Cの3段落に分かれています。以下のステップに沿って進めましょう。

STEP 1 英文を読み、段落ごとにタイムを計りましょう。読むのにかかった時間とWPM（1分あたりに読める語数）を右の **Speed Records** に記録しましょう。

STEP 2 英文を再度読みましょう。段落を読み終えるごとに、右の問いに答えましょう。

 59 words 🎧 DL 084 ⊙ CD2-28

Have you ever heard of the word "diversity?" It means many different types of things or people being included in something. In a global society, it is necessary to build an environment where people from different nationalities, genders, ages, and religions can work together. Rakuten is one of the first companies in Japan that
5 has tried to facilitate diversity.

 85 words  🎧 DL 085 ⊙ CD2-29

People were surprised at the news that Rakuten announced in 2010. It decided to use English as the official language of its company. By doing that, Rakuten became able to recruit excellent people from many different countries. In fact, people from more than 100 countries or regions work for Rakuten and easily
10 communicate in English. In the employee cafeteria, where employees can eat for free, you can see many menus for various cultures and religions. Also, there is a special room for them to pray.

 107 words   🎧 DL 086 ⊙ CD2-30

Rakuten not only builds a diverse environment, but also emphasizes creating a corporate atmosphere of working as a team. In working collaboratively with
15 people from various backgrounds, it is essential to have employees understand the company mission and head for the same goals. Rakuten talks about those goals at the all-staff meeting held every Monday and at an orientation for new employees. What's more, employees have chances to participate in cross-cultural exchange events. They learn about cultural differences in religious events, business
20 manners, and so on. Rakuten is trying to open a new future with the mission of "Empowering society and people through innovation" with diverse ideas.

Speed Records

A	59 (語数) ÷ _____ (かかった秒数) × 60 (1分あたり) = _____ wpm
B	85 (語数) ÷ _____ (かかった秒数) × 60 (1分あたり) = _____ wpm
C	107 (語数) ÷ _____ (かかった秒数) × 60 (1分あたり) = _____ wpm

A

1. ダイバーシティは特殊な能力を持つ人やものの集まりですか。　　　　（はい・いいえ）
2. グローバル社会ではどんな人々が一緒に働く環境をつくることが重要ですか。

   a. さまざまな国籍や性別の人々　　**b.** さまざまな趣味や特技をもつ人々
3. 楽天は何の促進にいち早く取り組んだ会社ですか。　　　　　（　　　　　　　　　）

B

1. 楽天は（　　　　　　　　　）を英語にすると2010年に発表しました。
2. 楽天は世界各国から人々を（　　　　　　　）し、現在（　　　　　　　　）以上の
   国と地域からの従業員が働いています。
3. 楽天の（　　　　　　　　　）にはいろいろな文化・宗教に配慮したメニューがあるほか、
   （　　　　　　　　）をするための特別な部屋もあります。

C

1. Rakuten wants diverse employees to also have diverse goals.　　**[T / F]**
2. Rakuten has an orientation for new employees every Monday.　　**[T / F]**
3. Rakuten supports its staff in learning about cultural differences.　　**[T / F]**

Dialog

A 次の会話を聞き、空所にあてはまる語を書き入れましょう。　🎧 DL 087　💿 CD2-31

Emma:　I think I'm **1.**(　　　　　) **2.**(　　　　　) **3.**(　　　　　) life in Japan, but I still don't know many things.

Kento:　Is something the matter?

Emma:　I learned the Japanese **4.**(　　　　　) "Circumstances may justify a lie" today at school. I have trouble agreeing that there are times when you can tell a lie.

Kento:　Oh, that means a lie that doesn't **5.**(　　　　　) anyone and makes things better can sometimes be necessary.

Emma:　Hmm …. Still, it is **6.**(　　　　　) for me to understand that. Is this phrase similar to *Honne to Tatemae*?

Kento:　Kind of. I guess Japan values the idea or atmosphere not to say things too directly.

B 次の1〜5のステップで、会話の発話練習をしましょう。

STEP 1　音読し、発音が分からない単語に下線を引きましょう。

STEP 2　**A**の音声をもう一度聞いて、発音を確認しましょう。

STEP 3　ペアを組み、EmmaとKentoになって読んでみましょう。

STEP 4　Emmaのみの音声 (🎧 DL 088　💿 CD2-32) を聞き、音声のスピードを意識しながらKentoのパートを発話しましょう。

STEP 5　Kentoのみの音声 (🎧 DL 089　💿 CD2-33) を聞き、音声のスピードを意識しながらEmmaのパートを発話しましょう。

Circumstances may justify a lie

Expression

A 日本語訳を参考に、英文を完成させましょう。

1. She goes to the church _____ every Sunday.

彼女は**お祈りをするため**、毎週日曜日に教会に行きます。

2. _____, there are people from _____ countries in this town.

実際、この街には**いろいろな**国の人々がいます。

3. The company will _____

this year.

今年、その会社は**100人の大学生を募集する**でしょう。

4. _____ around me.

私は私の周りの**人々に力を与えたいです**。

B 楽天について自分の意見を書いてみましょう。

What's your view on Rakuten Group?

I think Rakuten is a/an _____ group

because _____.

地方の商店に対する想い

　1997年2月、楽天の前身であるエム・ディー・エムが設立され、3カ月後に楽天市場が開設されました。同社はたった6人の従業員でスタートしました。当時はインターネットで買い物をすることもまだ珍しい時代でした。当初からインターネットショッピングを行うと決めていたわけではなく、実は、アメリカにあるパン屋のフランチャイズ展開なども候補の一つでした。しかし、この先のインターネットの可能性を信じ、地方の商店が集まるインターネット空間を作りたいという情熱と「日本を元気にしたい」という想いのもと、楽天はオンラインショッピングへの道をスタートしたのでした。

2023年時点で、約5.7万の店舗が出店している楽天市場ですが、開設時の出店店舗は何店舗だったでしょう？

a. 3
b. 13
c. 23

Unit 12

Amazon
STEM教育の充実を目指して

Small Chat

右の語句を参考に、次の問いに答えましょう。

Do you like shopping in stores or on the Internet?

1.

What kind of things do you usually buy online?

2.

What school subject do you find interesting?

3.

shopping online

books

science

clothes

shopping in person

art

Words and Phrases

 DL 090 CD2-34

A 次の日本語に合う英語を（　　）内に書き入れましょう。

1. 本社　　　　　　（ h _ _ _ _ _ _ _ _ _ _ _ _ ）

2. ガレージ　　　　（ g _ _ _ _ _ ）

3. 女子の、女性の　（ f _ _ _ _ _ ）

4. 分野　　　　　　（ f _ _ _ _ ）

5. 最も低い　　　　（ l _ _ _ _ _ ）

6. 調査　　　　　　（ s _ _ _ _ _ ）

7. 協働する　　　　（ c _ _ _ _ _ _ _ _ _ _ ）

8. 雇用　　　　　　（ e _ _ _ _ _ _ _ _ _ ）

9. 視点　　　　　　（ v _ _ _ _ _ _ _ _ ）

10. ～を探る　　　　（ e _ _ _ _ _ _ ）

B 次の語句に合う日本語訳を選択肢から選びましょう。

1.	at first	( )	**a.**	〜を表す
2.	stand for 〜	( )	**b.**	最初に
3.	major in 〜	( )	**c.**	〜を専攻する
4.	gender gap	( )	**d.**	リーダーシップ指針
5.	leadership principle	( )	**e.**	男女格差

Dictation

DL 091　CD2-35

音声を聞いて空所を埋めましょう。その後、英文を日本語に訳しましょう。

1. The founder started his business in a house (　　　　　　).

_____

2. The number of (　　　　　　) students in science (　　　　　　) is small.

_____

3. The motto teaches us the importance of (　　　　　　) (　　　　　　)

possibilities.

_____

Pre-knowledge

アマゾンについて調べ、次の1〜3が正しければT、間違っていればFを選びましょう。
調べた際に、新たに知ったことがあればメモ欄に書き留めましょう。

1. When it started, Amazon sold only electronic devices.　　　　[T / F]

2. The Future Engineer Program is one of Amazon's STEM education programs.

[T / F]

3. Amazon offered an online event called "Girls' Tech Day" in Japan in 2020.　[T / F]

Speed Reading

次の英文はA～Cの3段落に分かれています。以下のステップに沿って進めましょう。

STEP 1 英文を読み、段落ごとにタイムを計りましょう。読むのにかかった時間とWPM（1分あたりに読める語数）を右の **Speed Records** に記録しましょう。

STEP 2 英文を再度読みましょう。段落を読み終えるごとに、右の問いに答えましょう。

A 60 words DL 092 CD2-36

Amazon is a worldwide company whose headquarters is in Seattle, Washington. Amazon started in a house garage about 30 years ago and sold only books online at first. Now, Amazon sells various products like electronic devices, baby goods, and food. Amazon, which has become a big company, also offers some
5 social activities, including educational support toward STEM for female students.

B 78 words DL 093 CD2-37

STEM stands for science, technology, engineering, and mathematics. These four fields are said to be essential for future society. However, the number of girls and women studying these four fields is less than that of boys and men. Especially in Japan, the rate of female university students majoring in science is the lowest
10 among the 36 countries in the OECD survey in 2021. Amazon has offered many events to make the gender gap smaller in the STEM fields.

C 111 words DL 094 CD2-38

Amazon has collaborated with an NPO group since 2020 and has held events called "Girls' Tech Day," which is for young female students to learn technology. Amazon wants girls from junior high school to university to have an interest in
15 science and engineering, and then think about future jobs. This event aims to create a society where anyone can seek their employment without considering gender. This event is based on the motto "Think big," which is included in Amazon's 16 leadership principles. The idea suggests that we should have broad and new viewpoints. Without limiting our ideas, we should explore various
20 possibilities to achieve great success. Now everybody, let's think big!

Speed Records

A 60（語数）÷ _____（かかった秒数）× **60**（1分あたり）= _____ wpm

B 78（語数）÷ _____（かかった秒数）× **60**（1分あたり）= _____ wpm

C 111（語数）÷ _____（かかった秒数）× **60**（1分あたり）= _____ wpm

A

1. アマゾンの本社がある都市はどこですか。 （　　　　　　　　）

2. アマゾンが創業当初から扱っているものは何ですか。
   a. 書籍　　**b.** 電子機器

3. どちらの学生に対するアマゾンの社会活動について書かれていますか。
   a. 男子　　**b.** 女子

B

1. （　　　　　　　）は将来の社会に重要な分野といわれています。

2. OECDの（　　　　　）において、日本は参加した36カ国中、理系女子の割合が
   （　　　　　）位でした。

3. アマゾンはSTEM分野における（　　　　　　　）を小さくするために多くのイベントを実施しています。

C

1. "Girls' Tech Day" is an event to sell computers to junior high school girls. **[T / F]**

2. Amazon hopes to increase the number of young women interested in science.

   [T / F]

3. "Girls' Tech Day" is based on Amazon's motto "Think big." **[T / F]**

Dialog

A 次の会話を聞き、空所にあてはまる語を書き入れましょう。 DL 095 CD2-39

Emma: Your brother goes to ABC Institute of Technology, right?

Kento: Right. He always says his campus life would be more fun if there were more girls in his course.

Emma: I heard that the rate of female students ¹·( ) ²·( ) engineering and technology is very low in Japan compared to countries in Europe.

Kento: Exactly. Most of my female friends decided to go to ³·( ) faculties when they were in high school. I don't know ⁴·( ).

Emma: According to a ⁵·( ), many Japanese female students don't think they are ⁶·( ) enough to study science.

Kento: Really? I feel many of my female friends do better than me in the science subjects.

B 次の１～５のステップで、会話の発話練習をしましょう。

STEP 1 音読し、発音が分からない単語に下線を引きましょう。

STEP 2 **A**の音声をもう一度聞いて、発音を確認しましょう。

STEP 3 ペアを組み、EmmaとKentoになって読んでみましょう。

STEP 4 Emmaのみの音声（ DL 096 CD2-40 ）を聞き、音声のスピードを意識しながらKentoのパートを発話しましょう。

STEP 5 Kentoのみの音声（ DL 097 CD2-41 ）を聞き、音声のスピードを意識しながらEmmaのパートを発話しましょう。

Expression

A 日本語訳を参考に、英文を完成させましょう。

1. NPO _____ non-profit organization.
   NPOは非営利組織**を表します**。

2. To have _____ is essential for _____.
   新しい視点を持つことが**将来の社会**にとって必要不可欠です。

3. Our company wants to _____

   science.
   当社は理系コース**を専攻する女子学生を募集し**たいと思っています。

4. _____

   is in Tokyo.
   そのゲーム会社の本社は東京にあります。

B アマゾンについて自分の意見を書いてみましょう。

What's your view on Amazon?

I think Amazon is a/an _____ company

because _____.

アマゾンの社名変更

　1994年、アマゾン創業時の社名はCadabraでした。マジックショーなどで聞き覚えのある「アブラカダブラ〜」という魔法の呪文に由来しているそうです。しかし、その音が「死体」を意味するcadaver（カダバー）という語に似ていることから社名を変更しました。社名を変更する際に、創業者のジェフ・ベゾスは辞書から「Amazon」という単語を選びました。この単語を選んだ理由はいくつかあるようですが、

世界で最大規模の流域面積を持つ南アメリカのアマゾン川にちなんだことが理由の一つでした。また、amazonのロゴの下に付いている矢印がaからzに伸びているのは、扱う品がa〜zまで何でも揃っていることを意味しています。

著名実業家であるアマゾンの創設者の一人ジェフ・ベゾスの大学時代の専攻は？

a. 電気工学
b. 経済学
c. 文学

IKEA

すべての人が平等に暮らせる毎日を

Small Chat

右の語句を参考に、次の問いに答えましょう。

> What's Sweden famous for?

1.

| absolutely |

> Would you prefer to work in a large company?

2.

| salary |

| the Nobel Prize |

| No, I wouldn't. |

> What's your top priority for work?

3.

| flexible work hours |

| the northern lights |

Words and Phrases

 DL 098 CD2-42

A 次の日本語に合う英語を（　　）内に書き入れましょう。

1. 機能的な　　(f _ _ _ _ _ _ _ _ _)

2. 手ごろな　　(a _ _ _ _ _ _ _ _ _ _)

3. 多様な　　(d _ _ _ _ _ _)

4. 貧困　　(p _ _ _ _ _ _)

5. 資格　　(q _ _ _ _ _ _ _ _ _ _ _ _)

6. 〜を整える　　(a _ _ _ _ _ _)

7. 従業員　　(e _ _ _ _ _ _ _)

8. 国籍　　(n _ _ _ _ _ _ _ _ _ _)

9. 管理職　　(e _ _ _ _ _ _ _ _)

10. 包括的な　　(i _ _ _ _ _ _ _ _ _)

B 次の語句に合う日本語訳を選択肢から選びましょう。

1. cooperate with ~   (   )   **a.** その上、同様に

2. in addition   (   )   **b.** ～と協力する

3. as well   (   )   **c.** ～にかかわらず

4. account for ~   (   )   **d.** 加えて

5. regardless of ~   (   )   **e.** ～の割合を占める

Dictation

🎧 DL 099   💿 CD2-43

音声を聞いて空所を埋めましょう。その後、英文を日本語に訳しましょう。

1. Many people in the world live in (   ).

   _____

2. The company recruits employees (   ) (   ) nationality.

   _____

3. Women (   ) (   ) more than half of all (   )

   in the company.

   _____

Pre-knowledge

イケアについて調べ、次の１～３が正しければT、間違っていればFを選びましょう。
調べた際に、新たに知ったことがあればメモ欄に書き留めましょう。

1. IKEA was founded in the 1940s as a small shop which sold food.   [T / F]

2. In 1953, IKEA adopted flat-pack furniture so that customers could easily carry it.   [T / F]

3. The first IKEA store in Japan opened in Tokyo in 2006.   [T / F]

Speed Reading

次の英文はA～Cの3段落に分かれています。以下のステップに沿って進めましょう。

STEP 1 英文を読み、段落ごとにタイムを計りましょう。読むのにかかった時間とWPM（1分あたりに読める語数）を右の **Speed Records** に記録しましょう。

STEP 2 英文を再度読みましょう。段落を読み終えるごとに、右の問いに答えましょう。

A | **60 words** | 🎧 DL 100 | ◎ CD2-44

IKEA is a Swedish company whose founder started his business at age 17 in 1943. In 1948, he started selling furniture, and then expanded internationally. IKEA offers functional furniture and other items at affordable prices. It says its mission is "To create a better everyday life for the many people." With this vision,
5　IKEA supports diverse life and work styles.

B | **77 words** | 🎧 DL 101 | ◎ CD2-45

For example, IKEA Japan supports single parent families by cooperating with NPOs. It is reported that many single parent families in Japan struggle with poverty, and many of them, especially single mothers, are part-time workers. In order to help them, it provided training programs to help them improve their
10　business skills and obtain qualifications. In addition, IKEA Japan tries to support their lifestyles by giving lectures about ways to arrange home offices and save on living costs.

C | **110 words** | 🎧 DL 102 | ◎ CD2-46

IKEA does a lot to support their employees as well. With their vision of "Diversity and Inclusion," IKEA makes an effort to produce comfortable working
15　environments in which employees can work equally regardless of gender, age, or nationality. For example, employees can decide their working hours depending on their lifestyles, and their working conditions are based on equal pay for equal work. In 2022, in IKEA Japan, women accounted for more than half of all management positions, which is much higher than the 9.4% average of female
20　executives in Japan. IKEA's vision of accepting individual diversity will hopefully be a great example for how to make our society more inclusive.

Speed Records

A 　60（語数）÷ _____（かかった秒数）× **60**（1分あたり）= _____ wpm

B 　77（語数）÷ _____（かかった秒数）× **60**（1分あたり）= _____ wpm

C 　110（語数）÷ _____（かかった秒数）× **60**（1分あたり）= _____ wpm

A

1. イケアはどこの国の企業ですか。 　　　　　　　　　　（　　　　　　　　）

2. イケアでは高価な商品が多く売られていますか。 　　　　　（はい・いいえ）

3. イケアの創設者が家具を売り始めたのは何年ですか。

　　a. 1943年　　　**b.** 1948年

B

1. イケアは（　　　　　　　　　）の家庭を支援しています。

2. イケアはシングルマザーの人たちに、ビジネススキルの（　　　　　　　　　）や
（　　　　　　　　）の取得を助ける研修プログラムを提供しました。

3. イケアは、ホームオフィスを整えて、光熱費を（　　　　　　　　）するための
（　　　　　　　　）を行っています。

C

1. IKEA makes sure to treat all its employees equally. 　　**[T / F]**

2. Employees are encouraged to have the same schedule as each other. 　**[T / F]**

3. IKEA Japan has more women in management positions than the average
Japanese company. 　　**[T / F]**

Dialog

A 次の会話を聞き、空所にあてはまる語を書き入れましょう。　　🎧 DL 103　💿CD2-47

Kento: I want to buy a stylish desk lamp at IKEA today. I bet it will boost my
1.(　　　　　　　　　　) to study.

Emma: Oh, there's a café in IKEA. Why don't we have lunch there? I'm **2.**(　　　　).

Kento: OK. Um …. Is there anything I can eat on the menu? I don't eat meat.

Emma: How about "plant balls"? They **3.**(　　　　) **4.**(　　　　) meatballs, but
they are called "plant balls" because they are a plant-based food made of
beans and vegetables.

Kento: Sounds **5.**(　　　　　　　　　) and healthy. They are also good for the
people who don't usually eat vegetables but need their nutrition.

Emma: I think that they are perfect for vegetarians, too. That's another way
IKEA supports individual **6.**(　　　　　　) in society.

B 次の1〜5のステップで、会話の発話練習をしましょう。

STEP 1 音読し、発音が分からない単語に下線を引きましょう。

STEP 2 **A** の音声をもう一度聞いて、発音を確認しましょう。

STEP 3 ペアを組み、KentoとEmmaになって読んでみましょう。

STEP 4 Kentoのみの音声（🎧 DL 104　💿CD2-48 ）を聞き、音声のスピードを意識しながらEmmaのパートを発話しましょう。

STEP 5 Emmaのみの音声（🎧 DL 105　💿CD2-49 ）を聞き、音声のスピードを意識しながらKentoのパートを発話しましょう。

Expression

A 日本語訳を参考に、英文を完成させましょう。

1. The shop offers good products at _____ prices.
   その店は良い商品を**手ごろな**価格で提供しています。

2. Employees can decide their _____.
   従業員は**その上勤務時間も**決めることができます。

3. We should respect each other _____.
   ジェンダーや年齢にかかわらず、私たちはお互いを尊重すべきです。

4. Male students _____
   _____.
   男子学生が**料理クラブの全メンバーの半分を占めていました**。

B イケアについて自分の意見を書いてみましょう。

What's your view on IKEA?

I think IKEA is a/an _____ company

because _____.

IKEAという社名が示すもの

　IKEAの企業カラーは創業者の出身国スウェーデンの国旗の色をモチーフにしています。ではIKEAという社名の由来は何なのでしょうか？　IKEA（イケア）という音は、日本人にはあまり耳慣れない響きかもしれません。スウェーデン語では「イケーア／イケーヤ」、英語では「アイキーア」と発音されます。IKEAという言葉は実際に存在する単語ではなく、ある言葉のイニシャルをつなげたものなのです。IとKはイケアの創業者、Ingvar Kamprad（イングヴァル・カンプラード）のイニシャル、そしてEは彼が育ったスウェーデン南部の農場、Elmtaryd（エルムタリッド）の頭文字に由来しています。

IKEAのAは何の頭文字に由来しているでしょうか？

a. イングヴァルが育った村の名前
b. イングヴァルの母親の名前
c. イングヴァルが通った学校の名前

Unit 14

Dyson

未来のエンジニアを育てるための大学

Small Chat

右の語句を参考に、次の問いに答えましょう。

> What chores do you usually do at home?

> 1.

| clean the floor |

| a new vacuum cleaner |

> In your room, how many electronic devices do you have?

> 2.

| three or less |

| do the dishes |

> What new electric appliance would you like to have?

> 3.

| a new fan |

| four or more |

Words and Phrases

DL 106 ◉ CD2-50

A 次の日本語に合う英語を（　　）内に書き入れましょう。

1. 〜を発明する　　　　　　　(i _ _ _ _ _)

2. 特許　　　　　　　　　　　(p _ _ _ _ _)

3. 進行中の　　　　　　　　　(o _ _ _ _ _ _ _)

4. 投資　　　　　　　　　　　(i _ _ _ _ _ _ _ _ _ _)

5. もがく、格闘する　　　　　(s _ _ _ _ _ _ _)

6. 資格のある、能力のある　　(q _ _ _ _ _ _ _ _)

7. 学費　　　　　　　　　　　(t _ _ _ _ _ _)

8. 不足　　　　　　　　　　　(s _ _ _ _ _ _ _)

9. 入学、登録　　　　　　　　(e _ _ _ _ _ _ _ _ _)

10. 革新的な　　　　　　　　　(i _ _ _ _ _ _ _ _ _ _)

B 次の語句に合う日本語訳を選択肢から選びましょう。

1. be concerned with ~   (   )   **a.** ～に申し込む

2. educational institution   (   )   **b.** ～を心配する

3. be engaged in ~   (   )   **c.** ～に従事する

4. for free   (   )   **d.** 教育機関

5. apply for ~   (   )   **e.** 無料で

Dictation

DL 107   CD2-51

音声を聞いて空所を埋めましょう。その後、英文を日本語に訳しましょう。

1. Students must submit their (   ) by the first week of April.

   _____

2. James Dyson was (   ) with the (   ) of engineers.

   _____

3. Many young people will (   ) (   ) a job at the company to join

   (   ) projects.

   _____

Pre-knowledge

ダイソンについて調べ、次の1～3が正しければT、間違っていればFを選びましょう。
調べた際に、新たに知ったことがあればメモ欄に書き留めましょう。

1. The cyclone vacuum cleaner "G-force" was first manufactured by a Chinese
   company.   [T / F]

2. James Dyson established an institution of higher education in 2017.   [T / F]

3. Dyson offers an award for innovative ideas that solve the world's problems.
   [T / F]

Speed Reading

次の英文はA～Cの3段落に分かれています。以下のステップに沿って進めましょう。

STEP 1 英文を読み、段落ごとにタイムを計りましょう。読むのにかかった時間と WPM（1分あたりに読める語数）を右の **Speed Records** に記録しましょう。

STEP 2 英文を再度読みましょう。段落を読み終えるごとに、右の問いに答えましょう。

A **59 words** DL 108 CD2-52

James Dyson founded Dyson in 1993 after he invented the cyclone vacuum cleaner "G-force," which was the first vacuum cleaner without a disposable paper bag. The company has also produced air purifiers, hairdryers, and electric fans without fan blades. With about 9,000 patent applications and the ongoing
5 development of new technology, Dyson contributes to society in many different ways.

B **84 words** DL 109 CD2-53

In 2020, Dyson announced a new 2.75 billion pound investment plan into developing new technologies and it tried to expand into new fields. Based in Singapore, England, and the Philippines, it is increasing the number of engineers in fields such as software, machine learning, and robotics. England has been struggling
10 to produce enough qualified engineers due to increasing tuition, which caused a decrease in the number of students. Concerned with the shortage of engineers, James Dyson started supporting education for further research and development.

C **119 words**  DL 110 CD2-54

Dyson established the educational institution Dyson Institute of Engineering and Technology in England in 2017. The students there attend classes to study
15 for two days a week, and for three days, they are engaged in actual work projects with the professional members of the company's project teams. Their education is provided for free, and students are paid for their time and work. The school has been so popular that more than 850 people applied for the 25 open positions in just the first year. From the first day of enrollment, the students are able to contribute
20 to the development of new technology. Focusing on the development of engineers and scientists, Dyson will continue to produce innovative and unique products.

Speed Records	**A** 59 (語数) ÷ _____ (かかった秒数) × **60** (1分あたり) = _____ wpm	
	B 84 (語数) ÷ _____ (かかった秒数) × **60** (1分あたり) = _____ wpm	
	C 119 (語数) ÷ _____ (かかった秒数) × **60** (1分あたり) = _____ wpm	

A

1. G-force に付いていないものは何ですか。 (　　　　　　　　)

2. ダイソンの扇風機には羽根が付いていますか。 (はい・いいえ)

3. ダイソンが取り組んでいることは何ですか。
   a. 新技術を開発すること　　**b.** 特許の審査をすること

B

1. ダイソンは、さらなる技術開発に向けて多額の費用の (　　　　　　　) 計画を発表しました。

2. 海外にも拠点を持ち、ダイソンは、ソフトウエア、機械学習、(　　　　　　　) の分野の (　　　　　　) を増やしています。

3. イギリスでは、大学の (　　　　　　　) が高騰したため、エンジニアが (　　　　　　) することを心配したジェームズ・ダイソンは教育の支援を始めました。

C

1. Students can gain real work experience at Dyson Institute. **[T / F]**

2. Dyson hired 850 students to work in their educational institution. **[T / F]**

3. Dyson develops innovation through supporting engineering students. **[T / F]**

Dialog

A 次の会話を聞き、空所にあてはまる語を書き入れましょう。　🎧 DL 111　💿CD2-55

Emma: Dyson's hairdryers are ¹·(　　　　　　　　　)! I want to buy one.

Kento: Me, too! Oh, did you know Dyson developed new headphones with an air purifier? According to this magazine, you can have clean air as ²·(　　　) as listen to music. That's such a Dyson-like idea!

Emma: Wow, headphones with a purifier? What an innovative product! I wonder why they added a purifying ³·(　　　　　　　) to headphones.

Kento: I heard that they were trying to solve the social problems, such as noise and ⁴·(　　　) ⁵·(　　　　　　　), in urban areas.

Emma: Interesting! I remember you said that you're thinking of becoming an engineer. Your dream may come true at Dyson someday!

Kento: I really want to be an engineer, and ⁶·(　　　　　) those types of wonderful products.

B 次の 1 ～ 5 のステップで、会話の発話練習をしましょう。

STEP **1** 　音読し、発音が分からない単語に下線を引きましょう。

STEP **2** 　**A**の音声をもう一度聞いて、発音を確認しましょう。

STEP **3** 　ペアを組み、EmmaとKentoになって読んでみましょう。

STEP **4** 　Emmaのみの音声（🎧 DL 112　💿CD2-56）を聞き、音声のスピードを意識しながらKentoのパートを発話しましょう。

STEP **5** 　Kentoのみの音声（🎧 DL 113　💿CD2-57）を聞き、音声のスピードを意識しながらEmmaのパートを発話しましょう。

Expression

A 日本語訳を参考に、英文を完成させましょう。

1. A university student _____ a new type of _____ glove.

   ある大学生が新しいタイプの**使い捨て**手袋**を発明しました**。

2. The university provides some classes _____ because of increasing

   _____.

   学費の増加により、その大学はいくつかの授業を**無料で**提供しました。

3. The company increased _____ engineers

   in order to _____.

   その会社は**革新的な製品を生産する**ために、エンジニア**の数**を増やしました。

4. The town _____

   _____.

   その町は**医師不足を心配しています**。

B ダイソンについて自分の意見を書いてみましょう。

What's your view on Dyson?

I think Dyson is a/an _____ company

because _____.

サイクロン掃除機の開発秘話

　ジェームズ・ダイソンは、大学で美術を学んだ後、工業デザイナーとしてデザイン設計事務所で働いていました。当時、ジェームズは購入したばかりの紙パック式掃除機の吸引力が落ちることに不満を抱きました。これは、掃除機にごみが溜まるとフィルターが目詰まりを起こし、吸引力が低下することが原因でした。

　ジェームズは、近所の製材所の屋根に設置されていたサイクロン型

の木くずの処理装置からヒントを得て、サイクロン技術を掃除機に応用できないかと考えます。その後、彼は自宅のガレージにて一人、5年の歳月を経て第1号の試作機を完成させました。

5年間の開発期間にジェームズ・ダイソンは何台の試作品を作ったのでしょうか?

a. 57台

b. 512台

c. 5127台

謝辞

　本書の制作にあたり、多大なるご協力及びご助言をいただきました以下の企業の皆様に感謝の意を表します。なお、本テキストで紹介している内容は、2023年8月時点のものです。

（掲載順）

株式会社セブン−イレブン・ジャパン

LINEヤフー株式会社

一般財団法人LINEみらい財団

日清食品ホールディングス株式会社

日本マクドナルド株式会社

公益財団法人ドナルド・マクドナルド・ハウス・チャリティーズ・ジャパン

ウーブン・バイ・トヨタ株式会社

トヨタ自動車株式会社

株式会社豊田自動織機

スターバックス コーヒー ジャパン 株式会社

イオン株式会社

株式会社良品計画

アップルジャパン

楽天グループ株式会社

アマゾン ウェブ サービスジャパン合同会社

イケア・ジャパン株式会社

ダイソン

※本テキストで紹介しているダイソンによって設立・運営された大学は、Dyson Institute of Engineering and Technology。

本書にはCD（別売）があります

Purpose
Companies for Social Good
英語で学ぶ社会における企業の存在意義

2024年1月20日　初版第1刷発行
2024年2月20日　初版第2刷発行

著　者　　原 田 寛 子
　　　　　土 屋 麻衣子
　　　　　Samantha Hawkins

発行者　　福 岡 正 人
発行所　　株式会社　金 星 堂

（〒101-0051）　東京都千代田区神田神保町 3-21
Tel　（03）3263-3828（営業部）
　　　（03）3263-3997（編集部）
Fax　（03）3263-0716
https://www.kinsei-do.co.jp

編集担当　四條雪菜・戸田浩平　　　　　　　　　Printed in Japan
印刷所・製本所／萩原印刷株式会社
組版／朝日メディアインターナショナル株式会社
本書の無断複製・複写は著作権法上での例外を除き禁じられています。本書を代行業者等の第三者に依頼してスキャンやデジタル化することは、たとえ個人や家庭内での利用であっても認められておりません。
落丁・乱丁本はお取り替えいたします。
ISBN978-4-7647-4199-7　C1082